THE LIBRARY OF HOLOCAUST TESTIMONIES

From Lwów to Parma

The Library of Holocaust Testimonies

My Lost World by Sara Rosen
From Dachau to Dunkirk by Fred Pelican
Breathe Deeply, My Son by Henry Wermuth
My Private War by Jacob Gerstenfeld-Maltiel
A Cat Called Adolf by Trude Levi
An End to Childhood by Miriam Akavia
A Child Alone by Martha Blend
The Children Accuse by Maria Hochberg-Marianska and Noe Gruss
I Light a Candle by Gena Turgel
My Heart in a Suitcase by Anne L. Fox
Memoirs from Occupied Warsaw, 1942-1945
by Helena Szereszewska
Have You Seen My Little Sister?
by Janina Fischler-Martinho
Surviving the Nazis, Exile and Siberia by Edith Sekules
Out of the Ghetto by Jack Klajman with Ed Klajman
From Thessaloniki to Auschwitz and Back
by Erika Myriam Kounio Amariglio
Translated by Theresa Sundt
I Was No. 20832 at Auschwitz by Eva Tichauer
Translated by Colette Lévy and Nicki Rensten
My Child is Back! by Ursula Pawel
Wartime Experiences in Lithuania by Rivka Lozansky Bogomolnaya
Translated by Miriam Beckerman
Who Are You, Mr Grymek? by Natan Gross
Translated by William Brand
A Life Sentence of Memories by Issy Hahn, Foreword by Theo Richmond
An Englishman in Auschwitz by Leon Greenman
For Love of Life by Leah Iglinsky-Goodman
No Place to Run: The Story of David Gilbert by Tim Shortridge and
Michael D. Frounfelter
A Little House on Mount Carmel by Alexandre Blumstein
From Germany to England Via the Kindertransports by Peter Prager
By a Twist of History: The Three Lives of a Polish Jew by Mietek Sieradzki
The Jews of Poznań by Zbigniew Pakula
Lessons in Fear by Henryk Vogler
To Live is to Forgive … But Not Forget by Maja Abramowitch

From Lwów to Parma

A Young Woman's Escape from Nazi-Occupied Poland

KLARA ROSENFELD

Introduction by BELLA GUTTERMAN,
Yad Vashem, Jersusalem

VALLENTINE MITCHELL
LONDON • PORTLAND, OR

First published in 2005 in Great Britain by
VALLENTINE MITCHELL
Suite 314, Premier House
Edgware, Middlesex HA8 7BJ

and in the United States of America by
VALLENTINE MITCHELL
c/o ISBS, 920 NE 58th Avenue, Suite 300
Portland, Oregon 97213-3786

Website: www.vmbooks.com

British Library Cataloguing in Publication Data

A catalogue record for this book has been applied for

ISBN 0-85303-603-9

Library of Congress Cataloging-in-Publication Data

A catalog record for this book has been applied for

Printed in Great Britain by Antony Rowe, Chippenham, Wilts

This book is dedicated to the memory, life and love of my beloved parents, brothers and sisters whose voices were forever silenced in the Holocaust.

To my esteemed and courageous savior Fosco Anoni, and his caring family.

To my late husband, who helped me craft this record of my memories and emotions, and provided support and strength throughout the process.
And to my dear children and their families, who made it all worthwhile.

A special thank you to Yad Vashem, and to Dr Bella Gutterman for dedicated research, assistance and guidance in the publishing of this book.

Contents

The Library of Holocaust Testimonies
  by Sir Martin Gilbert   *ix*

Introduction: Historical Background
  by Dr Bella Gutterman   *xi*

1 Life Under the Soviets   1

2 German Occupation   14

3 The Italians   25

4 The August *Aktion*   32

5 The Ghetto   44

6 Escape   83

7 To Italy   103

8 The Convent   131

The Library of Holocaust Testimonies

Ten years have passed since Frank Cass launched his Library of Holocaust Testimonies. It was greatly to his credit that this was done, and even more remarkable that it has continued and flourished. The memoirs of each survivor throw new light and cast new perspectives on the fate of the Jews of Europe during the Holocaust. No voice is too small or humble to be heard, no story so familiar that it fails to tell the reader something new, something hitherto unnoticed, something previously unknown.

Each new memoir adds to our knowledge not only of the Holocaust, but also of many aspects of the human condition that are universal and timeless: the power of evil and the courage of the oppressed; the cruelty of the bystanders and the heroism of those who sought to help, despite the risks; the part played by family and community; the question of who knew what and when; the responsibility of the wider world for the destructive behaviour of tyrants and their henchmen.

Fifty memoirs are already in print in the Library of Holocaust Testimonies, and several more are being published each year. In this way anyone interested in the Holocaust will be able to draw upon a rich seam of eyewitness accounts. They can also use another Vallentine Mitchell publication, the multi-volume *Holocaust Memoir Digest*, edited by Esther Goldberg, to explore the contents of survivor memoirs in a way that makes them particularly accessible to teachers and students alike.

Sir Martin Gilbert
London, April 2005

Introduction: Historical Background

On the eleventh day of the Second World War, the armies of Germany stood at the gates of Lwów. However, the Molotov–Ribbentrop pact, which partitioned Poland into a German-occupied zone and an area to be possessed by the Soviet Union, forced the Germans to retreat to the San River – bringing eastern Galicia (the eastern part of Poland) under the yoke of Soviet rule. When the Germans evacuated the area and the Soviet army entered Lwów, about 10,000 Jews fled from the city to Hungary and Romania. A few even returned to the German-occupied zone due to fear of being under communist dominion. This marked the beginning of a new era in eastern Galicia, the German threat having been deflected by the more concrete threat of communist rule.

The Soviets took possession of 47,000 square kilometers of eastern Galician territory, including a population of about 600,000 Jews. Some 100,000 of these Jews were refugees who had fled eastward a short time earlier in fear of the approaching Germans. The Soviet takeover of eastern Galicia led to immediate radical changes in public administration, the social and political structure, and the constellation of daily life. Political and community frameworks that were perceived as hostile to Soviet interests were dismantled and the Jews were forced to disband their traditional institutions and organizations, including the basis of Jewish public life, the *kehilla* (community administration). Youth organizations and Zionist political parties were also abolished. Many Jews were arrested and interned in prisons and detention camps, and others were forced to go underground.

In late November 1939, orders for the socialization of land

and industry were issued. Private property, factories, and businesses were nationalized, and many of those who were arrested in this context – on suspicion of being members of the 'bourgeoisie' and owners of property – were Jews. For those who were associated with the new regime, in contrast, it was a time of celebration. They received key appointments in the Soviet bureaucracy and were placed in high-level economic posts.

Due to its location, Lwów had always been an important commercial crossroads where many national minorities – Ukrainians, Poles, Germans, Russians, and Jews – lived side by side. The city, a cultural center for the area since the seventeenth century, housed many institutions of science and the arts: the University of Lwów with its well-stocked library, the Polytechnical Institute of Lwów, and a clutch of well-known schools and cultural institutions that attracted many of the finest artists of Poland to the town's theaters, opera, and art galleries. The city also had historical sites of great interest, including numerous Jewish community buildings and synagogues. The Jews' contribution to the town was vast and perceptible and their community was the third largest in Poland, following Warsaw and Łódź. The Jewish community of Lwów was vigorously involved in culture and creative endeavor. The town hosted the Yiddish theater of the famous actress Ida Kaminska, and provided a series of renowned Jewish literary figures with a rich source of inspiration. Intensive Jewish involvement was also evident in science and law.

On the eve of the war, about 100,000 Jews lived in Lwów, out of a total population of 700,000. When the war began and during the era of Soviet rule, the Jewish population of the town doubled in size. In the spring of 1940, when the Soviets exiled 50,000 Jews to the Russian interior after invoking a regulation that forbade foreigners to live near the border, 190,000 Jews remained.

The German invasion and the violation of the German–Soviet accord resulted in mass imprisonments in Lwów, mostly of Ukrainians who belonged to nationalist parties. The pretext for the mass arrests was the Ukrainians' decision to embark on an overt uprising against the Soviets. The Ukrainians established fortified rooftop positions and took potshots at Soviet soldiers who were making a panicky retreat, leaving behind huge quantities of weapons and ammunition. Concurrently, the Soviets began to evacuate their civilians in an operation fraught with difficulties. Most of the evacuees were Communist Party loyalists, practitioners of crucial occupations, and people in circles associated with the authorities. They were joined by some 10,000 Jews, mainly young people affiliated with leftist circles, army officers, and those whom the regime considered essential. Jews who attempted to follow them into the Soviet Union were sent back to the German-held territories.

The Soviet evacuation from Lwów lasted five days, and the more panicky it was the more emboldened the Ukrainians became. They did not flinch from assaulting individual Russian soldiers, stealing ammunition that had been deposited, and burgling shops and warehouses.

UKRAINIAN RIOTS AT THE ONSET OF THE GERMAN OCCUPATION

When the Soviets pulled out of Lwów on 28 June 1941, they left behind three lockups filled with prisoners, including Jews. In the last days of their rule, the authorities killed most of them and buried them in the prison courtyards and cellars. Most of the internees were political prisoners.

When the Germans entered Lwów on 28 June an impassioned and patriotic Ukrainian population awaited them, envisaging the establishment of an independent Ukrainian state. The slogans that the Ukrainians chanted – 'Beat up the Jews and the Communists', 'Long live Stefan Bandera!'[1] Long live Adolf Hitler!' – revealed the hopes that they had pinned on the Germans. Residues of traditional ancient anti-Semitism made them willing to take part in the mistreatment and murder of Jews during the first days of the German occupation. Yellow-and-blue Ukrainian flags were unfurled alongside the German flag, the Soviet star was taken down, and the prison courtyards filled with relatives who came to find out what had become of the internees. The spectacle of the heaps of corpses precipitated an additional wave of violence, again aimed at the Jews. The bodies of about 3,000 prisoners, including those of four German pilots whom the Soviets had taken prisoner, were found in the courtyards and cellars.

The next day the Germans, with the fervent participation of Ukrainians, began to abduct Jews to clean the prisons and bury the dead. The Jews engaged in this labor for four days. Concrete floors were smashed; bodies were hauled out of the cellars and removed for burial. Others were taken to cemeteries as prey for cruel and monstrous abuse and were shot as a large crowd of Ukrainians and Poles stood and watched. The rabble, goaded by the Germans, argued that it was the Jews who had denounced the internees. The fact that many of those killed were Jews, including about 200 members of Zionist pioneering youth movements, was immaterial; no one heeded the voice of reason. The false version of events won the day and was disseminated among German soldiers and members of Einsatzgruppe C,[2] who operated in Lwów and had been brought there to witness the murderous actions personally. One of the Germans wrote that the Ukrainian population had undertaken a 'laudable' action against the Jews in the first hours after the Bolsheviks had left. In their rampage against the Jews of Lwów, they seized about 1,000 of them and hauled them to the prison. Police captured and shot about 7,000 Jews in retribution for the inhuman acts of brutality. The Jewish victims included a group of well-known public figures, academicians, and journalists, such as Henryk Hescheles, editor of the newspaper *Chwilla*, and Rabbi Ezekiel Levin, rabbi of the Progressive congregation in Lwów.

The riots waned four days later, allowing the Jews to entertain the faint hope that the storm had blown over. They had prepared themselves for hard and dangerous years and realized that they would be left to their own devices. However, even the experience of centuries of violence did not suffice to prepare them for what awaited them now. Indeed, they were given no respite whatsoever. The mayhem this time emanated not from its direct perpetrators, the Germans, but from their Ukrainian lackeys. The Germans had learned how to exploit their Ukrainian underlings, who on their behalf struck the first blows, stunned and confused the Jewish public, turned the Jews into a persecuted mass, and rocked the foundations of their existence. After they had brought this phase about, the Germans came on the scene and, with the help of decrees and laws, restored the appearance of order and calm.

The next blow to the Jews of Lwów began on 20 July with the 'Petliura days'.[3] During this terrible period, Jews were forsaken by their neighbors and friends, captured, and – after incessant abuse – executed. Thus the Ukrainians chose to commemorate their leader, the Hetman Semyon (Simon) Petliura, who had been shot by a young Jew.

After five days of rioting, the Germans reclaimed the reins of authority and indicted the Ukrainian rioters. The city calmed down. The quiet, however, was not meant for the Jews. The Germans had decided to torch all the ancient synagogues of Lwów, including the famous Turey Zahav (Golden Rose) Synagogue, a magnificent specimen of Gothic art that had been designed by an Italian architect and built in 1582.

On 22 June 1941, the day of the German invasion, Ukrainian nationalists convened in Kraków and proclaimed the establishment of an independent Ukrainian state, on the basis – they claimed – of an explicit German promise. This statement made such an impact that it prompted the Metropolitan Szeptycki to welcome and thank the Germans in a broadsheet that called for 'obedience to the regime and the orders of the authority, which do not clash with the laws of God'.[4]

On 17 July, by decision of the Führer himself, eastern Galicia became a district of the Generalgouvernement. Its name from the days of the Austro-Hungarian Empire –

Galizien – was reintroduced and Lwów was designated its capital. All the Jewish laws that had been gazetted in the Generalgouvernement were now applied to the Jews of Galicia, including the armband regulation. The Galician version of the armband had a blue Star of David against a white background. This marking, reminiscent of the benighted Middle Ages, prompted the Jews of Lwów to seek ways to evade the stricture and its implications. Some went so far as to arrange a hasty out-conversion, but even this method proved disappointing as the anti-Semitic press abounded with articles excoriating priests for their willingness to allow the Jews to evade their intended fate.

When the annexation of Galicia to the Generalgouvernement was completed, the German combat units were evacuated, a civil administration was established in their stead, and the combat troops were replaced with soldiers in service units, including some composed of Italian and Hungarian forces. Ten days later, Hitler signed orders concerning the organization of German authorities in the East, including an order for the establishment of a civil administration in the occupied territories.

On 1 August 1941, however, the bureau of the governor-general, Hans Frank, issued a directive that obliterated the name 'Western Ukraine', and the next day the Germans carried out a series of arrests among Ukrainians who had held key positions during the first days of the occupation. A ceremony repealing the independence of 'Western Ukraine' took place at the former Sejm building. Hans Frank, who attended the ceremony, stressed the Führer's wish to return Galicia to the orbit of Greater Germany. The Ukrainian militia that had been established after the Germans came in was also swiftly dismantled, but only after it was praised for having aided and cooperated with the Germans. A Ukrainian auxiliary police force under German command was established to replace the militia. 'Attempts to resist', the nationalist circles were warned, 'will be punished in accordance with the emergency laws.'

As the Ukrainian episode wound down, the civil administration of Galicia District steadily took shape. The first civilian governor was Dr Karl Lasch. SS-Gruppenführer Fritz Katzmann was appointed SS and police commander in eastern Galicia.

Officially, Katzmann reported to the district governor, but in fact he reported directly to the SS and police commander in the Generalgouvernement, Gruppenführer Friedrich Krüger, who was based in Kraków. Katzmann brought his staff with him, resulting in the formation of two parallel hierarchies of command: the Civil Administration, charged with reactivating the city, and the SS staff, which amassed power steadily.

The staff included Untersturmführer Anton Lönert, inspector of Jewish labor at the labor camps in Galicia; Untersturmführer Heinz Seyss-Inquart, Katzmann's adjutant; Erich Engels, head of the Jewish Affairs office of the Gestapo, who had come from Warsaw, where he had been a special duties officer; SS Sturmbannführer Stawicki, commander of the criminal police; and Dr Wagner, who ran the SS economic departments in Galicia. Additional Germans made their appearance: many SD and SS units that set up headquarters in Lwów, members of Schupo (Schutzpolizei, conventional police) and Kripo (Kriminalpolizei, criminal police), and, in their wake, workers of Organisation Todt, who began to prepare the area for the exploitation of the Jewish labor force. A unit of Italian soldiers who had fought alongside the Germans also stationed itself in Lwów.

CONCENTRATION OF THE JEWS OF LWÓW AND ESTABLISHMENT OF THE JUDENRAT

The Germans began to press the Jews of Lwów immediately after the end of the Ukrainian rampage. The second blow that they inflicted the Jews, after the 'Petliura Days', was an act of economic warfare. The German administration announced the imposition of a fine ('contribution') of 20 million roubles against the Jewish population in order to revitalize the city after the ravages of the siege and the battles. The penalty caused great dismay in the Jewish street, raising fears that the Jews would not be able to collect so large a sum without a central guiding body. After all, the *kehilla* institutions had long been non-existent. Again, however, the Jews proved able to mobilize when in need and to take action when the fate of the entire Jewish population was at stake. Most Jews regarded the imposition of the fine as the end of their nightmare. The new regime, as terrifying as it was, seemed willing now to content itself with economic extortion, a practice to which Jews had been accustomed for generations. The Jews rushed to the building of the Judenrat, which had just been established by order of the Germans. Women donated jewelry, many Jews sold their property for half its value, and the affluent made large donations. The peasants in the vicinity feasted on the offerings. Knowing that the Jews had no choice, they swarmed into Lwów and snapped up everything available in the Jewish streets, which had become one large fair.

As the fine was being paid, the city remained calm and the Jews were not harmed. Afterwards, the Judenrat used the rather large sum that remained in its coffers to make various payments. The Germans augmented the economic pressure by collecting furniture and houseware for themselves. To systematize this operation, the Judenrat established a special supply department to meet all the demands of the German administration as well as those of private German civilians, who regularly appeared at the offices of the department to demand valuables such as furniture, sets of dishes, and clothing.

Another way to attack the Jews was reflected in the method of distributing food, the supply of which progressively dwindled. Rationing was imposed in Lwów and the ration cards stipulated the commodities that were to be distributed. Jews were placed at the bottom of the ladder and were allotted one-fourth the quantity of food that Germans received. Thus it is no wonder that a black market began to flourish in the Jewish street, as it did in all of Lwów. Katzmann used the occasion to blame the Jews as the perpetrators of the illicit commerce.

It was during those days of economic decrees and expropriation that Lwów acquired the first of its four Judenräte. The background for the establishment of the Judenrat was the immediate need for some central body that would coordinate all activities related to the lives of Jews under the occupation regime. The Germans, in turn, considered the Judenrat a mediator for the implementation of their directives and a tool for the attainment of their ultimate goal. They ordered the Ukrainian mayor to enter into a discreet dialogue with Jewish leaders regarding the establishment of the Jewish council. The mayor, Dr Polanski, contacted important Jewish personalities and negotiated with them. The council was formed rapidly, but a problem arose in appointing a chairman. The Germans demanded that the council be headed by a person of repute and public stature. They chose Professor Mauricy Allerhand, a well-known attorney and jurist who had served on the Supreme Court, written books on the law and justice, and served for some time as dean of the University of Lwów law school. However, Allerhand turned down the offer and the mayor returned to the Germans empty-handed. Several weeks later, Allerhand was arrested in one of the first *Aktionen* and put to death. The search for a chairman evoked fear in the Jewish street as the names of candidates circulated by word of mouth. The Gestapo signaled its growing impatience, and on 22 July 1941, seven days after the promulgation of the arm-band order, City Hall proclaimed the establishment of the Judenrat under the leadership of Dr Joseph Parnes. His deputy was Dr Adolf Rothfeld and the two were joined by five additional members. Dr Parnes vacillated about the appointment at length, but eventually accepted it when he realized that the Germans were about to lose patience and respond in a way that would be adverse to the entire Jewish population.

In the meantime, the rioting and pillage during the first days of the German occupation had paralyzed the city and its industrial plants, most of which had been run by Jews. The SS and police commander in the Generalgouvernement, Gruppenführer Friedrich Krüger, in conjunction with the military authorities, decided to put the Jews back to work. On 20 September an order signed by the town's civilian authorities mandated compulsory labor for every Jew aged 14–60. The directive expanded the labor regulations that had been introduced in the Generalgouvernement in October 1939 to include Jews in the areas that had been occupied from the Soviet Union and annexed to the Generalgouvernement. In practice, this constituted the implementation of a directive to concentrate the Jews in special neighborhoods and camps as a phase in the process of rendering Europe *Judenrein*. Until that could be accomplished, it allowed the Reich to exploit the Jewish labor force for its own purposes. Pursuant to the directive, a special labor bureau established in the Jewish residential district placed the Jews in jobs and the Judenrat was held responsible for the performance of the directive.

An important department of the Judenrat, to which appointments were prized, was the Judische Ordnungsdienst Lemberg, the 'Jewish order service' or the Jewish police of Lwów. In the initial organizing phases, a need was felt to establish a Jewish order service in the quarter. The official directive for the formation of the Jewish police in Lwów was handed down on 8 November 1941, by the SS and police commander in Galicia District, but the practical organizing work had begun in August of that year. The force was allotted a quota of 500 policemen. To train them, a commander of the Jewish police in the Warsaw ghetto was brought in, but the Jewish policemen in Lwów, unlike those in Warsaw and elsewhere, did not receive special uniforms. Their main identifying mark was a cap, taken from the warehouses of the Polish police, on which a Star of David marked with the initials J.O.D. appeared instead of the Polish eagle emblem. In addition to the cap, the policemen wore a yellow band on the left arm and carried rubber batons. The force was tasked with kidnapping Jews for service in labor camps, the establishment of which had begun in September–October 1941. Although the police were ostensibly considered an arm of the Judenrat, they took their orders from the German authorities and, for the most part, directly from the Gestapo. The Jewish police had a difficult task to perform. Their connection to the Judenrat became weaker and weaker, and their human profile changed. If at first young members of the intelligentsia and members of youth movements joined the Judische Ordnungsdienst in order to avoid service as unskilled laborers, these people soon proved unable to withstand the psychological burden that their duties entailed and were replaced by others who were less sensitive and, at times, by criminal elements. The fact that policemen had broader entitlements than the rest of the Jewish population, including larger food rations, was a powerful magnet for individuals who flinched from nothing in their struggle for survival. At the time of the sealed ghetto, the number of Jewish police came to 750.

ESTABLISHMENT OF THE JEWISH QUARTER AND ORGANIZATION OF THE JEWISH LABOR FORCE

The Labor Department was an institution of vast importance from the day compulsory labor was proclaimed.

The Jews always perceived the Germans' actions and decrees as rigid and immutable. Their attempts to postpone the deadline for the payment of the 'contribution', to prevent abductions in the streets, and to thwart the removal of Jews to labor camps, did not work out well. 'I won't give Jews', Dr Parnes told the Germans when he was ordered to deliver quotas of workers for the camps, and he was taken away for execution – after which a wave of abductions ensued.

On 8 November 1941, an order signed by Dr Lasch, the civilian administrator of Galicia District, announced the establishment of a Jewish quarter – *Judische Wohnbezierk* – in the Zamarstynów and Kleparów neighborhoods of northwestern Lwów. A detailed map of the city and the district was attached to the order. Many homes in the designated areas lacked provisions for sewage, water, and electricity. Most were clay hovels; a few were made of stone. The neighborhoods were separated from the rest of town by railroad embankments. It was a supremely appropriate area for a district that would be isolated from the rest of the city. According to the order, the Jews were given two weeks to move there. The homes that they were to evacuate, especially those in the center of town, were to be included in a neighborhood that was earmarked for Germans.

Many Jews rushed to obey the order. Hurriedly they hunted for places to live, wishing to obey the new directive quickly and spare themselves further assaults. The displacement and relocation process, harsh to begin with, was accompanied by the so-called '*Aktion* under the Trestle'. It was at this strategic location – a railroad trestle at the only entrance to the Jewish quarter – that Ukrainians and German SS men stationed themselves and mercilessly beat and assaulted all persons who came and left.

The 'resettlement' *Aktion* lasted until December, as the Judenrat members made strenuous efforts to postpone the deadline in order to give the Jewish population time to organize and find places to live in the small slum district that had been reserved for them. Many Jews did not move and remained in their apartments in the center of town. Amazingly, the Germans did not apply the relocation order vigorously. The quarter was not sealed. The decree remained on the books but nothing was done to enforce it. At this stage, it seemed, the Germans were content with the torment of the displacement and the victims they caught. Furthermore, December 1941 and January 1942 were relatively calm months; apart from an isolated economic stricture known as the *furs Aktion*, the Jewish community calmed down and took a breath of relief. For the time being, the Germans did not wish to alarm the Jews because this might lead to unrest. The assaults against the Jews were reduced to very small-scale *Aktionen* that were meant to erode the Jewish community from within, to isolate it from the surroundings, and to weaken it until it was totally helpless. Thus each small-scale *Aktion* was followed by an ostensible respite that was meant to lull the Jews and reinforce their hope that each *Aktion* was the last of its type and that some form of *modus vivendi* with the Germans could yet be worked out. Hence the Germans did not assault the Jewish population at large in one stroke. At first, they attacked defenseless groups, weak groups, and elements for whom the community was willing to disregard attacks.

Deportations, transports, and killing *Aktionen* in Lwów began in March 1942. In February of that year, the second chairman of the Judenrat, Dr Adolf Rothfeld, died of natural causes and his deputy, Dr Henryk Landsberg, was appointed in his stead. Dr Landsberg was a temperate and compliant chairman who explained his obeisance by noting that 'We are living in totally different times today. Our community [administration] is no longer a religious one [like the traditional *kehilla*] but rather an instrument that carries out the Gestapo's [wishes]'. Officer Engels of the SS, who tasked the Judenrat with preparing the lists and carrying out the evacuation, set a quota of 33,000 persons who would be deported in 33 trains escorted by Jewish police and doctors. Judenrat officials were sent out with lists to assist the Jewish police. Three days into the *Aktion*, the Germans, dissatisfied, took over from the Judenrat and carried on for about three weeks. Some 15,000 Jews were deported from Lwów. The *Aktion*, also known as the 'March *Aktion*', ended two weeks before Passover, and afterwards the remaining Jews were re-registered, issued with new ID cards and labor permits, and reclassified. They were marked and sorted into two categories. One was vital workers (A [Arbeiter – worker] Jude), each of whom received a new armband with an embroidered serial number and a registration certificate (*Meldkarte*) and was allowed to add another person from his or her household. The others were classified as H (Haushalt – household) Jude. An announcement signed by the director of the labor office in

Lwów, on 20 April 1942, stated that all other labor permits would henceforth be invalid.

The situation in Lwów eased somewhat in the April–June 1942 period. Small-scale *Aktionen* did take place, in which, for the most part, several hundred Jews were removed to the camps. These numbers, however, seemed insignificant to the Jews of Lwów. After all, how important was the fate of 900 people who had been evacuated from one street or another and taken to the Janowska camp in comparison with tens of thousands of Jews who were still able to carry on with their daily lives and fight for their shaky existence? In one of many *Aktionen* that took place during the afternoon hours in June 1942, a segment of a street in the Jewish quarter was sealed off and about 900 Jews were removed to the aforementioned camp. The 'veterinarians *Aktion*' and the 'insurance agents *Aktion*' also occurred during these months. These operations, however grim they were for the Jews, did not disrupt the ordinary course of their lives; the people who had been taken to the camp vanished into the hordes of other prisoners. The Jewish community and the decision-makers in the Judenrat believed that Jews who could demonstrate their usefulness for the German military effort would be able to survive. This is the background tor the establishment of the Judenrat's large labor enterprise, the 'municipal workshops'. The shops were staffed by some 3,000 Jews, who bought their own tools and machinery and brought them to the workplace. Additional civilian and military plants where Jews could hold jobs and qualify for the treasured labor permit were established. In the summer of 1942, however, overall responsibility for Jewish affairs was transferred to the SS, which considered the Civil Administration too weak to control the chaos in 'labor relations'. Quick action was needed, Katzmann noted. Employers were intervening on the Jews' behalf too often for Katzmann's taste, and this intervention, in his opinion, was unsuited to the German spirit and honor. After looking into the matter, the SS commanders claimed that the tailoring and haberdashery workshops were worthless in wartime. They felt the same way about other enterprises, where thousands of Jewish shift laborers collected scrap metal and renovated uniforms.

AKTIONEN AND DEPORTATIONS FROM LWÓW

In June 1942, the Jewish population decreased steadily. The *Aktion* that month was a grim portent of what was to come. Carried out by an itinerant SS killing unit (*Rollbrigade*) under Officer Engels of the SS, the twelve-hour *Aktion* also involved the evacuation of some prisoners from the Janowska camp. During the same month, representatives of the SS, the police, and the Generalgouvernement administration attended a working meeting in Kraków for the purpose of preparing plans for *Aktionen*. In the minutes of the meeting, the representatives of the various districts reported on the Jewish population in their respective areas of control and described how they intended to expedite the solution to the Jewish question. In this exchange, Katzmann detailed the measures that had been taken in regard to the situation in Galicia:

> Most of the Jews in Galicia District have been evacuated [*evakuiert*] in large numbers. At this time, 85,000 Jews are living in Lemberg, 45,000 of whom are employed in a labor process. More Jews will be evacuated [*ausgesiedelt*] in the next few weeks.

This report implies that half of the 160,000 Jews who had been in Lwów at the outset of the German occupation were no longer alive in June 1942. Some had been killed in riots and small *Aktionen*, others had died of starvation and disease, and the rest had vanished in the labor camps. June–September 1942 were the peak months in terms of the magnitude and intensity of the *Aktionen*. In Lwów, too, these were the hardest months for the Jews of the town and the camp. In the middle of July, on the eve of the Ninth of Av, a committee of German bureaucrats visited the Ruhstof plant and restamped all the labor permits – a measure that always presaged distress and catastrophe. Rumors about a new *Aktion* spread quickly, and the Jews' prayers on the fast day were accompanied by passionate entreaties and wailing. Several days later, the Germans, following their standard practice, began to restamp documents in other enterprises but used a different method and different criteria. Nothing happened after the stamping; life seemed to revert to its familiar routine. An ill omen appeared in early August 1942: Lwów was preparing for an important visit, on which occasion the Jews were forced to clean and festoon the town. The Germans convened in Lwów, in an augury of preparations for an *Aktion* of exceptional severity and scale. Indeed, they took the first step immediately after the conference ended: they dissolved the labor bureau that they had established and sent the Jewish clerks away. As the parting proceeded, Heinz Weber told the Jews: 'Henceforth the Jewish question will no longer be an economic problem; it will be solved from a political point of view only.' The town was quarantined and ringed by army guard units. The SS *Rollbrigade* arrived again. The *Aktion* began on 10 August 1942, after abductions in the streets and the dissemination of false rumors about its timing. As part of the preparations, warehouses had been readied at the Czwartków camp in the center of town for the gathering of the Jewish property.

The murder operations began with the killing of medical personnel and patients in the ghetto hospitals. The *Aktion* continued for ten days without interruption, during which about 50,000 Jews were taken to Janowska and Belzec.[5] Then the Germans stopped the *Aktion* for two days in order to deceive the Jews and lure them from their hideouts. The moratorium was well planned; during its course, some of the SS men who perpetrated the *Aktion* were sent to peripheral towns, where they busied themselves liquidating small ghettos and sending their inhabitants to Belzec and Janowska. Escape *en route* to Janowska was impossible due to the stringency of the SS and askar guards. The only chance was to leap from the train on the way to Belzec. Jews aboard the trains attempted with their fingernails to create an opening in the grille of the car. Even jumping from the train, however, gave no assurance of salvation. Most Jews who attempted it were injured or were struck by the guards' bullets. Some of those who managed to evade these hazards reached the ghetto, where they went into hiding. Eventually this path to salvation was also blocked because the Germans began to strip their victims before making them board the trains.

The *Aktion* resumed on 22 August and now included employees of the municipal workshops. Most of them were taken to the camp, where the able-bodied were interned. Trams packed with hundreds of standing Jews rumbled along the city streets for two days. The detainees were taken to the Janowska camp, where they were sorted for transport to Belzec. The 'August *Aktion*' ended on 24 August. The Germans used those final days to tie up loose ends. They abducted children who had been left in the Jewish quarter without relatives, gathered them at the post office, and transported them from there to the camp. The tragic culmination of the *Aktion* was the arrest and public hanging of Dr Henryk Landsberg, chairman of the Judenrat. The Jewish quarter fell into desolation, entire streets depopulated. The brutalities seemed to have exceeded even the Germans' norm. Evidence of this appears in a report of 16 October 1942, by a representative of the Civil Administration:

> The *Aktion* for the transfer of the Jews sometimes takes place in ways that are so unbefitting of a civilized people that they invite a comparison between the methods of the Gestapo and those of the GPO, Stalin's secret police. The railroad cars that are used for these transports are said to be so decrepit that Jews who wish to escape from the transport cannot be stopped. The result is that wild gunfire and manhunts erupt from time to time at the railroad stations on the way... Although the German population and the entire non-Jewish population are

convinced about the need to eradicate all the Jews, it would be advisable for these extermination actions to be performed in a way that does not evoke such amazement and displeasure.

THE DEATH THROES OF THE LWÓW GHETTO

On 21 August 1942, several days before the August *Aktion* ended, an order concerning the establishment of a Jewish ghetto in Lwów in a small part of the Jewish quarter was issued. Nine of its clauses described the boundaries of the ghetto and restrictions pertaining to leaving it. This time the order was signed by Katzmann, giving further confirmation of the fact that the strategy was purely political and that the economic motive, weak to begin with, had vanished altogether. The Jews were given until 7 September 1942 to move into the ghetto.

The ghetto area was severely cramped. It was bordered from the south by a massive railroad embankment, from the west by barren hills, and from the north by orchard areas, where the trees and shrubs tempted Jews to escape but were patrolled by guards. To the east, the ghetto was bordered by the city proper. The ghetto was encased in a wooden fence, for which the Jews paid. The fence had three gates, but only one of them was used for passage. Germans and Ukrainians stood outside the fence and members of the Jewish police circulated inside. Individuals were not allowed to leave; only work companies had this privilege. The second gate was meant for wagons and cargo; the third was used only when persons abducted in *Aktionen* were to be loaded onto the trams.

On 1 September 1942, even before the ghettoization deadline, the Germans launched a campaign of intimidation and terror after a German soldier was killed at the Czwartków camp in Lwów. In the course of the punitive *Aktion*, SS men drove up to the Judenrat building in trucks and began to drag the employees out.

On 7 September, the deadline for moving to the ghetto, a new Judenrat began to operate under Dr Landsberg's deputy, Dr Eduard Eberson, who served until February 1943 and did the Germans' bidding without any bargaining ability whatsoever. By this time, the Germans had no need to camouflage their actions. About 50,000 Jews remained in the ghetto and the echoes of gunfire were continually heard from the Janowska camp. Dr Eberson did not delude himself and acknowledged his bitter plight: 'Even if I do not want the position, I must accept it as a disciplined member of a Zionist party, even though I know full well that the risk of death awaits me.' The Jewish population of Galicia was plummeting. In a re-registration for the issue of ration cards, only 36,000 persons were enumerated. About 15,000 waived their entitlement to bread cards in order to avoid registration.

The intensity of the extermination actions eased slightly in the autumn and winter of 1942/43. For the Jews of Lwów, however, there was no respite. Three small *Aktionen* took place during this time: on 18 November, on 5 December, and on 5 January. The November *Aktion* occurred shortly after a re-registration that the authorities had proclaimed. In this procedure, the Jews of the ghetto were sorted on the basis of their membership in one of two groups – R, denoting Rustung Industrie, or W, Wehrmacht. About 12,000 persons received new permits and were housed in barracks in the ghetto. The others, from that moment on, were deemed to be unneeded and were sorted out for death in the next *Aktion*. After the registration, 15,000 Jews were killed in a limited *Aktion*, reducing the ghetto population to 30,000.

In the January 1943 *Aktion*, Dr Eberson and the other members of the Judenrat were taken to Janowska and the ghetto was downscaled and redefined as a Julag (a *Judenlager*, Jews' camp). The change came about as the result of a decision by Himmler to transform ghettos that still existed into labor camps. The Julag area was small. The prisoners were concentrated in barracks and, by order of Katzmann, 'were housed temporarily, quarantined in the Jewish residential area'.

Military discipline was imposed in the camp and the construction of a new wooden fence begun. The Julag was divided into two sections that were differentiated by the status of their inhabitants.

The SS command in Lwów also underwent changes. Katzmann left and was briefly replaced by Gruppenführer Jürgen Stroop, the subsequent liquidator of the Warsaw ghetto. An SS officer named Mansfeld was placed in charge of the Julag, assisted by his adjutant, Siller, who came from the Janowska camp. The last commanders were Josef Grzimek and his deputy, Hainisch. SS men replaced the members of the Deutsche Wache (German Guard), who had been relatively benign. The internees were allowed to exit the Julag in organized groups only, and each enterprise that employed them had to assign an 'Aryan' official to escort them to the plant and back.

In May 1943, Katzmann returned to Lwów to finish the job that would earn him the expression of gratitude from Himmler for having made Galicia *Judenfrei*. When he arrived, on 25 May 1943, the signal for the liquidation of the Julag was given. All 1,200 shift workers at the Schwarz and Co. works, who until then had been considered immune from any depredation, were killed on the camp premises. Two days after this *Aktion*, on 31 May, the liquidation of the Julag itself began. The Germans had been informed by their agents about an important change that had occurred among the remaining Jews in the Julag and realized that the camp would not be obliterated without a struggle. According to the information they had received, the Jews had built bunkers and acquired weapons that they intended to use. This is indeed what happened when the Germans set out to liquidate the Julag on 31 May 1943. The *Aktion* proceeded with much difficulty as the internees put up resistance including the use of firearms. Shots were fired at the Germans from various positions, impeding their progress. In one location a group of young Jews barricaded themselves in and barred the Germans from the alleys. At this point, the Germans eschewed overt combat and began using methods that had proved themselves in the Warsaw ghetto. They brought barrels of fuel into the Julag and began to blow up the buildings systematically, one by one. Katzmann's report describes these measures in detail, with no effort at concealment:

> Indeed, additional immense difficulties arose at the time of the *Aktionen*, because the Jews tried to evade the evacuation at any price. Not only did they attempt to escape but they hid in all sorts of corners that are difficult to imagine – sewage trenches, chimneys, and even cesspools. They fortified themselves behind barricades, in underground passageways, in cellars that had become bunkers, in holes in the ground, in sophisticated hideouts, in lofts, and inside pieces of furniture.
>
> As the number of remaining Jews decreased, their resistance escalated. They defended themselves with weapons of all kinds, especially those of Italian origin. The Jews had purchased these weapons from the Italian soldiers who were garrisoned in the district for large sums of zloty ...
>
> Special methods were needed to liquidate the Jewish residential quarter in Lwów, where the aforementioned bunkers had been set up. Here, to prevent losses to our side, it was necessary to act brutally from the outset – several buildings were detonated or destroyed by fire. *En passant*, it was found, surprisingly, that instead of the 12,000 Jews about whom we had been informed, 20,000 were captured ...

This was the last *Aktion* in Lwów in which Katzmann took part. The German command held him responsible for the difficulties that had arisen during the final liquidation. After he wrote his summarizing report on the solution of the Jewish question in Galicia District, he was appointed SS and police commander in Gdansk, where he stayed until the end of the war.

Thus the curtain fell on Galician Jewry generally and the Jews of Lwów in particular. This account of their lives in the ghetto is merely background information for the story of the hardships and horrors that awaited them at the Janowska camp.

Bella Gutterman
Yad Vashem, Jerusalem

NOTES

1. Leader of the Ukrainian nationalists. In February 1940, he caused the movement to split and become radicalized. Shortly before the German invasion of the Soviet Union, he aided the Nazis and established two Ukrainian battalions for intelligence purposes. He proclaimed Ukrainian independence on 30 June 1940, but was interned in Sachsenhausen in September 1941.
2. Special mobile SS and SD units that accompanied the Wehrmacht in the 1939 invasion of Poland and the 1941 invasion of the Soviet Union. Officially, their mission was to eliminate political opponents. In the Soviet Union, they engaged mainly in mass murder, particularly of Jews.
3. The riots were depicted as acts of vengeance to mark the anniversary of the death of Semyon Petliura, the last prime minister of independent Ukraine, who was shot in Paris by a Jew on 25 May 1926.
4. Andrej Szeptycki (1865–1944), Metropolitan (head) of the Greek Catholic Church in southeastern Poland and a leading figure in the Ukrainian nationalist movement in Poland. Born into the Polish nobility, he had lengthy and good relations with Jewish community leaders and even promised to restrain the Ukrainians' murderous actions. Concurrently, however, he displayed a pro-German political orientation.
5. Belzec: an extermination camp in eastern Poland.

1 Life Under the Soviets

I went to the shopping district on Legionów Street to buy
some things. On the way, I studied the shop windows, paying
no attention to the crowds on the street. All of a sudden, I
heard airplanes overhead, blaring sirens, and the whistling of
falling bombs. Panic-stricken people ran into buildings and
sought shelter in the stairwells, their faces reflecting horror.
The planes cruised above the houses, their terrific noise
making people's blood freeze. Every second seemed to last an
hour. The bombs sounded as if they were all flying in our
direction. Several people in my shelter fainted; others cried.
One resident of the building came over and told us what the
radio had announced: a war had begun and the Germans
were invading Poland. My only wish now was to be at home
with my family. Come what may, I wanted to be with them.

Soon the planes disappeared, the sirens sounded the all-
clear, and I went out to the street. I found streetcars
overturned, hundreds of people lying dead or wounded,
ambulances racing to and fro, and panic everywhere. On my
way home, I saw people gathering on street corners, listening
to a broadcast. I stopped for a while to listen. The Polish radio
was announcing that a war was on; German forces had
crossed our border. We would fight for every part of our
country and not surrender our soil to the invaders. The British
government promised help. It would send planes and armed
forces to assist us. There was no immediate mobilization; only
the regular army was fighting on the front lines. I ran all the
way home, anxious to be there.

I found the whole family together and happy that I was
back. They asked me what was going on in the center of town,

and I told them everything I had seen. As we were talking, my brothers made a decision: they would pack up and head for the Soviet border[1] the next day. The Germans were taking away our young people, we were told. The whole town was in an uproar because all the young people were leaving. The next day was a very unhappy one for our family, since my brothers were going away.

The German army advanced into Poland. The British help never arrived. Fifteen years old and ignorant of evil, I did not know what war meant. In my imagination, a war was something fought by armies on a battlefield, as I had learned in history class. When I grew up, I thought, I would adopt the words my father used to say: 'before the war' and 'after the war'.

The front lines had already advanced to the outskirts of Lwów. We sat in the best shelter we had, the cellar. The German air force was bombarding the town heavily, not only in the center but all over. Whenever the planes disappeared, we ran out of the cellar to see where the bombs had landed and what damage they had done. One of the bombs exploded in front of a three-story building near our cellar, leaving a deep hole and shattering the water mains. The water supply to our building was cut off. We had to walk several blocks away to a pump, fill buckets with water, and haul them home.

There was already a long queue at the pump. As I approached the front of the line with my buckets, German planes passed over several times and we had to run for shelter. By now we feared not only bombs but also bullets. The planes were passing very low overhead and firing machine guns at anyone they spotted. Within a few days, it became impossible to be in the street. The front had moved into the suburbs of our town and bullets whizzed over our heads.

The last three days of the fighting were especially horrible. We spent them sitting in our shelter, trembling and afraid. Nobody dared to go out. Three o'clock in the morning was the quietest hour; it was then that Mother went home to prepare food.

The shooting stopped after those three horrible days, and we could not understand why. Some people suggested that it was only a brief intermission. Others felt that someone should go out to the street and see what had happened. One man volunteered. He came back quickly, yelling joyfully that we could come out, that the Soviet army had come to our rescue.

Our first response was disbelief. However, when we ran into the street we saw Soviet soldiers on trucks, some distributing food to the population and others singing cheerful songs and playing instruments. They were followed by huge double-decked tanks full of soldiers that stopped at various places in town. The population stood around them, agape. Nobody had known that such things existed, let alone seen them. I took them for invincible mobile fortresses.

We went back to our homes and my brothers returned the next evening. One night, I went out with a girlfriend for a walk. Soviet soldiers were singing and dancing on every street corner, talking to everyone, and trying to convince us how good it was in Russia.

The next day, the streets were full of refugees from German-occupied areas. The Germans had captured all of Poland up to Przemyśl.[2] Half of Lwów was under German occupation; the other half was under Soviet occupation. The streets were packed with women, children, and especially men, all seeking shelter in the Soviet-held area. They all thought it would be temporary only and that later they would be able to return to their families. Most of them had nowhere to go and nowhere to eat and sleep. Wishing to help these unfortunates, we took one family with children to our house. Most of the refugees, we found out, were Jews who were afraid to stay under the Germans. Life in our town slowly returned to normal.

The Soviets took over the government. They brought Communist Party members from Russia, who organized everything according to their methods. They opened factories, shops, schools, and other facilities. They and their secret police, the NKVD,[3] purged all offices of undesirable elements.

Every day we heard about people who had been arrested – officers in the Polish army, leaders of political parties, nationalists, and important Zionists. Many of our friends, afraid to stay at home, fled to the villages and went into hiding. The Soviets issued an order requiring every person above 16 years of age to apply to the police for an internal passport. Applicants had to submit brief autobiographies. Refugees from out of town did not receive passports unless they were specialists in certain trades; otherwise they were merely registered.

The next Soviet order was that anyone who had left his or her home and family and wished to return had to register in a certain office. Many refugees in our town had left their parents, wives, and children back home. Now, unable to find work in our town, they registered as the Soviets had instructed. They were told to be in a certain place at a certain time. When they showed up, they were surrounded by Soviet police, loaded into railway cars, and taken to Siberia.

One day, the radio announced that the Red Army would be carrying out anti-aircraft exercises for the next three days and everyone was to stay at home and off the street. This came upon us suddenly; nobody knew what it meant. The next day, we found out: it was a ruse. Russian militiamen and NKVD agents went from house to house at night, arresting all the refugees and transporting them deep into Russia. We felt tremendous pity for these unfortunates. We expected to receive word by mail from the family that stayed with us, but nothing came. We knew nothing of their whereabouts. Nor did we know that the refugees would be better positioned to survive in the Soviet interior than those of us who remained in Lwów.

My friends Ada and Rena and I decided to find work. We signed up with an employment agency and waited a long time to hear from them. Eventually Ada was hired as a telephone operator and Rena as a cable clerk, but I was still waiting for a suitable position. My father occasionally met a Russian man at a tailor's shop who introduced himself as the director of a new office that would be opened shortly. The office would need new clerks, the man said. My father replied that he had two daughters who were seeking jobs. The next day, my sister Hela and I went to the office and found people already waiting. We had to write brief autobiographies, which the secretary took from us, and we were told to return in two hours. We strolled through town to pass the time. When we returned, my sister and another girl, the tailor's niece, were hesitant about entering first. They sent me in, and as I entered the secretary hired me on the spot. She told me later that the director had asked her to employ the first candidate who entered her office. As it turned out, the secretary had liked me from the first moment she saw me, had hoped that I would be the first to enter, and was glad to have me with her. My position was statistical clerk.

I started work at nine o'clock the next morning. During my two-hour lunch break, I would walk home, just a few blocks away. It was not my habit to knock on the door of our house or open it delicately. Instead, I would fall into the house like a hurricane. There was a small room near the kitchen, in the middle of which was our large dining table with chairs around it. By the time I came, the whole family would already be seated for lunch. Hela, my older sister, always asked me, 'Can't you enter like a human being, instead of a ghost driven by a tail wind?' 'It's none of your business,' I would answer. With that, she was ready immediately to quarrel with me or to hit me. She was more like a boy than a girl. She was smaller than I, even though she was older. This gave her a complex of sorts: she was always angry with me, and Mother had to step in and settle things between us.

I was always in a hurry. Mother knew that my entire lunch, tea and all, must be on the table. I would finish everything quickly and go back to work. When I came home from work at three o'clock in the afternoon, it would happen all over again. Every other evening I would visit my boyfriend, Fred, or my girlfriends Ada, Rena, and Eva.

I felt splendid at the office. I liked my work and the

5

managers liked me and were very pleased with me. One day, I saw a weekly bulletin pinned on the bulletin board. An article in it, written by the manager, mentioned me by name, expressed gratitude for my satisfactory work, and assured me that a raise in salary would follow shortly. A couple of months later, the staff was cut back severely and three older clerks were laid off. I was the only one left on the job, although the others had seniority and academic education. The manager said that my abilities gave me great potential and that he would not let me get by with mere secretarial work because that would deny me a chance to advance.

One evening, my girlfriends and I went to Jezuicki Park. Ada and I left at 9.30 p.m. because I had to be at home by ten o'clock. Father enforced the curfew by closing the gate from the inside and securing it with a safety latch at exactly that time.

We lived in a one-story house surrounded by a large lot where we grew flowers and fruit. The house itself was set back far from the street and enlosed by a tall fence. Whenever I came home late, I had to climb over the fence. As Ada and I left the park, two boys, Fred and Poldek, approached us and accompanied us home. As we walked, they asked us out for the next day. At the last moment, Poldek motioned me aside with him and told me privately that Fred might not come tomorrow because he had already made a date with somebody else and would be busy.

The next day, Ada told me that Fred seemed to be a very nice boy and that she liked him. I liked Fred, too – I had from the first moment I had seen him, in fact – and for that reason we decided not to meet the boys in case Fred didn't come. Instead, we went to the sports club, sure that we would not encounter them there.

They were to meet us in a different section of town, near the Church of St Anne. We spent time at the club playing checkers and we bought cigarettes to smoke later somewhere else. This was due to Ada's influence on me. She had grown up without a father and always wanted to do adult things.

Suddenly, we heard a voice from behind: 'Does Klara's

father allow her to smoke cigarettes?' I blushed deeply. It was the son of one of our neighbors. Later, he said that he knew me very well, although I did not know him. He then sat down at our table and we passed the rest of the evening very nicely. A short time before we left, Fred and Poldek showed up at the club but didn't even look in our direction. We had the impression that they were angry at us for having broken the date. We left the club and walked to the park together with another group. After a short while, I looked at my watch and saw that it was time for me to go home. Anxious to get home before 10.00 p.m., I took my leave quickly and boarded the first streetcar that I saw.

The car was overcrowded, as it usually was at this time. When the conductor came around to me and I started to pay the fare, someone from behind called out that he had already paid for me. When I turned to see who it was, I saw to my amazement that it was Fred. Seeing me leave the club, he had followed me and climbed aboard the same streetcar. Fred was a tall, handsome boy, and when I turned around to see him, I had to look up. When our eyes met, we both started to laugh. Instead of hopping off the streetcar at my stop, I stayed with Fred until we reached the terminal and then he accompanied me back home. Father had latched the gate by then, so I asked Fred to climb over the fence and open it for me. He hesitated, knowing that we had a large dog who barked incessantly, but eventually he jumped the fence very easily. I liked the way he did it. I thanked him and started to say goodnight. Instead of letting me go, he asked what plans I had for Sunday. We decided to go together with Ada and Rena to a hill in the nearby Kleparowski forest to sunbathe. I thanked him again and ran into the house. Ada and Rena were glad that I had asked him to come with us.

When Sunday came and Rena and Ada did not show up, I went to the forest alone. It was a busy place; lots of people went there on weekends for picnics and sunbaths. Nearby was a rifle range that was usually used by the army. When I reached the appointed meeting place, I found only Fred.

Later, I found out that Rena and Ada had stayed away deliberately in order to honor a rule that we had concluded long ago and that I had forgotten: if one of us met a boy she liked, the others would stay out of her way and let her spend time with him alone. Thus, Fred and I went off by ourselves. On subsequent occasions, we would meet in the evenings and share the day's events.

Fred had a job at the local airfield and earned a decent salary that usually burned a hole in his pocket within a day or two. He simply could not keep money. He would buy sweets, drinks, or various other things for all his friends. When he was totally broke, I paid for his movie tickets and streetcar fares when we went out. We went to movies once or twice a week or sometimes just walked through the crowded streets of our town. At first, Fred told me that he was a refugee from the German-occupied part of Poland and, like many others, had escaped to Russian-occupied Lwów. He said this to make me think he was Jewish. He even mixed Yiddish words into our conversations. However, he could not maintain the masquerade for long. One day, while we were on the streetcar, he gave me his picture and asked me to read the inscription on the back. There, I read, 'To Klara, with love, Alfred Gwozdziewicz.' Only a Christian would have such a name. He had learned those Yiddish words from Jewish friends. As I read the inscription, he watched my facial expression to gauge my reaction upon finding out he was not a Jew. I thanked him for the picture and put it in my purse. Fred was greatly relieved, having overcome a moment that he had feared. He had thought I would break up with him the minute I knew he was not Jewish. It was nothing for me; I had suspected it for some time. His faith made no difference to me as long as I liked him.

However, the issue created trouble at home. My parents, although educated people who had many non-Jewish friends in town, were old-fashioned and would never allow me to date this boy. Once, when I had often been seen with a particular boy, my father called me aside and asked who he was. I lied and made up a name. Father believed me but noted that some of our good friends who had seen us together thought he might be a Christian. My whole family opposed my going out with that boy. Now, even my cousin Shulem, a friend of Fred's, told me to stop dating him.

Of all seven children in our family, I was the second youngest and the youngest girl. Only my brother Max was younger. Imek, my oldest brother, was already married to a woman named Klara and lived in a furnished apartment. Having a family of his own, he did not care about anything or anyone in our family, including me. Adolf, the second brother, was tall, dark, and very intelligent, always interested in books. He was also married and lived in a furnished apartment but spent most of his time in our home, like a second father. He showed me special kindness, always wanting to know who my friends were, whom I was dating, and even what dresses I wore. Filip, my third brother, was a tall, blond fellow who was always hanging around business people and always had money. He could afford to buy furniture for our sister Cill when she married her boyfriend, Zigi. The Soviet army drafted Zigi shortly after they were married and stationed him in Leningrad. Hela, Cill's twin sister, had learned to be a dressmaker. She loved movie stars and spent all her free time in cinemas. I was the sixth child. Max, the youngest, attended Pedagogie High School. He was a very intelligent boy who liked his studies.

All the children, even those who were married and lived separately, spent most of their time at our home. On Saturdays and holidays, the whole family gathered for meals and to be together. Our parents took great pride in this. Whenever we sat together around the table, people criticized me, saying that I did not like to help out with the housework and that I was always out. Indeed, I was different from my sisters. I kept more to myself and never liked to talk about myself. The sibling to whom I was closest, and with whom I shared my problems, was Max. Even he, however, sometimes called me stupid and empty-headed because I never had the patience to listen to his stories and his lessons from school, which he tried to explain to me. He was a born teacher.

Cill and Hela always had secrets between themselves. Whenever I mentioned anything to them, they shushed me, saying, 'You're little'; 'You don't understand'; or 'You don't know.' They took classes in a dance school before the Soviet occupation and got new tailor-made dresses. For me, there was always an old dress that could be altered to fit or that was too small for the others. I was only sixteen; Cill and Hela were twenty. Nobody noticed that I was also growing up, and nobody even tried to understand me. Adolf ordered me to leave the room whenever my sisters had boyfriends over. When I was in the room, he said, they always paid more attention to me and invited me to be with them. I was well developed for my age, well built, tall, and blonde. People mistook me for Hela, Cill's twin.

When I met Fred, I felt a kind of security, the sense that somebody was waiting for me and that I meant something to someone. He was tall and broad-shouldered, and I always felt good in his presence. I never told him what was going on in my house, but sometimes I mentioned that my parents would not agree to our dating regularly. Whenever I saw a member of my family in the street – especially my brother Adolf – I ducked into the nearest residential building and waited until he or she was out of sight. After a short time, Fred got used to it.

Several times we decided not to meet again, but wherever I was, Fred always found me. I spent free evenings with Ada when she was on duty at the telephone exchange. Fred knew this and came into the building to look for me late in the evening. Sometimes he found me with Rena or waited for me near the streetcar terminal until I got there on my way home. Once he told me that I had spent two hours watering the flowers and doing other odd jobs in our yard and garden. He had spent all that time in a building across from ours, watching me and waiting for me to go out. Although we had agreed to break up, we could not help ourselves. We resumed dating and were very happy.

One day, as we walked near Sax, an office where people registered for marriage, he proposed that we go in and register. Naturally, I turned it into a joke and then we both laughed. We were very happy together and I didn't want to concern myself about our future. Fred was always proud of me and tried to demonstrate this whenever he had a chance. When we went to the cinema, he pushed people aside to make room for me to pass. When the way to our home was muddy, he picked me up and carried me across, over my protests.

As 1940 drew to a close, we celebrated New Year's Eve in a café. Eleven of us – four girls and seven boys – went to a few places until we found one with some empty tables. Rena was with her cousin Muki, and Ada, Runa, and I were with Fred. It was the first time in my life that I was out very late. We had a wonderful time. Everybody had a bag of confetti and we threw them at each other.

Muki asked me to dance a tango with him. It was the first time I had danced and Muki, with his good humor, emptied his whole bag of confetti on my head and my dress. When we went back to our table, I realized that Fred was very angry. He wouldn't talk to anybody. I was sure he was a bit drunk. When a friend of my sister's approached and asked me to dance with him, Fred restrained me. I didn't understand him, but Ada called me aside and told me that Fred was jealous because I had danced with Muki. Besides, she liked Muki very much; they started to go out together after that. When we left the café, Fred admitted that my behavior had put him in a very bad humor. I promised not to flirt with anybody again. All ended well; we wished each other a happy new year and departed happily. None of us could imagine the disaster that 1941 would bring.

It was a very frosty winter. I caught a cold one morning and felt so bad that I could hardly get up and go to work. I forced myself out of bed and went to the clinic to see a doctor, who diagnosed a severe cold but didn't want to give me a note to excuse me from work. I begged him, but he explained that I didn't have a high fever. I was concerned, since the Russian officials punished anyone who missed a day's work without a medical excuse or some other form of permission. When I came to work the next day, the secretary, Geni, asked me if I had a note. She was also worried because without the note I might be hauled in front of a court and punished. I told her not to worry; I would get one. After lunch, I told the story to my father, who went to the clinic, consulted a doctor friend, and asked him to intervene. Together they went to the doctor who had examined me and proved to him that I was really ill. With that, he wrote out the note. Geni was very relieved; had the outcome been different, she would have had to report that I had missed a day's work without sufficient excuse.

Coming to work late, even by 30 minutes, was also severely punished. Once I was late because my clock at home had been slow. Geni waited until I arrived and then issued my tag. She also risked punishment for having waited for me, since it meant submitting her daily report later than usual. I explained to my superiors that I had been discussing some work problems with the secretary.

The winter passed and spring was in the air. I was very happy. In the office we discussed the preparations for the 1 May ball. My mother spent nearly a whole day waiting at a store to buy material for two new dresses for me. One was red; one was blue. They had to be ready for my birthday on 1 April. One day, toward the end of April, several high-ranking Russian officials visited our office. One of them, a short, thin, well-dressed man, came into the room where I worked, sat down near me, and spoke to me about my work. He said that he had heard of my good work and knew that I would receive a bonus. I was unmoved; I knew the Russians liked to pay compliments and I was one of the youngest girls in the office. After he left, my manager asked me, 'Do you know to whom you were speaking just now?' When I answered in the negative, he told me, 'That was the Minister of Trade and Commerce, Mr Kaganovitz.'

On 1 May we had a big parade, with all the workers in

Lwów taking part. Flags and portraits of Soviet leaders were everywhere. The ball was held that evening, and I had a great time.

2 German Occupation

A couple of weeks later, on a sunny Sunday morning, we woke up suddenly to the sound of gunshots and heavy vehicles rolling past our house. From our windows we saw Soviet tanks and trucks moving in the direction of the border. The streets were crowded and the news spread like lightning: the Germans were attacking the Russians. I dressed and ran to my brother Adolf's apartment. I woke Adolf up, told him the news, and asked him to come to our house at once. He didn't believe me. Then I ran to my brother Imek with the news. He laughed, saying it was only maneuvers by the Russian army. Two hours later, the whole family gathered at our home. Adolf did not even have a chance to say goodbye, because when he went out to inquire if he had to enlist, he was drafted on the spot and was not allowed to return. Imek received a call from the army to enlist immediately; so did Filip. Rachel and Klara, my sisters-in-law, stayed with us. Cill was with us, too, because her husband Zigi was stationed in Leningrad.

We heard gunfire from the windows and roofs of several houses. Ukrainian nationalists[4] had organized in groups to shoot at the Soviet troops on their way to the frontier. Nobody knew at the time how it happened that two organized sides, the Ukrainians and the Soviets, were fighting each other. Nobody was allowed to stand near a window or in the street. Russian NKVD agents fired at anyone they saw, guilty or not. We soon learned that several good acquaintances of ours had been shot merely because they were standing near windows. Fred raced to our home and stayed with us in case we needed help; he wanted to protect me.

After three days of this, we saw the Soviet forces retreating in total disarray. Many civilians also left Lwów in the direction of Russia. The roads were blocked by refugees and were bombed by the Nazis several times. Filip came home because he had encountered Imek and Adolf among the retreating forces and didn't want his sisters and parents to be alone and helpless in case something happened.

The German army entered Lwów over the next few days. The Ukrainian nationalists came out of hiding. Their young people had special tags pinned to their breasts bearing their national emblems and small blue-and-yellow flags. They helped the Germans loot the shops and then began shooting in all directions.

We lived in terrible fear. Nobody dared to go out the house; we could only hope that things would calm down in a few days. My father, who had already survived one world war as a soldier in the Austrian army, suffered from melancholy and nervous stress. He was afraid of everything.

After the regular army came the Gestapo.[5] Specially trained groups launched pogroms in the streets. Life itself became unsure; no one who stepped out of his home knew whether he would be able to return to his family. The invaders removed all males from their homes, concentrated them in certain places in town, and told them they were taking them away for labor. None of them ever came home again. The first job they had to do was cleaning the prisons, which were full of corpses. They were probably political prisoners who had been killed by the retreating Soviet forces and left there for weeks. The whole town stank from the smell of those corpses and the dirt. They chose the most intelligent people for this work, including Rabbi Levin,[6] the chief rabbi of Lwów, whom the entire population respected and loved. Some of the laborers were beaten to death while working; the survivors were taken out of town and shot to death by the Gestapo. Several of our neighbors were killed in the street when they went out to get some food for their starving families. The Ukrainian nationalists, sure that Hitler would free the Ukraine and return it to them, hung their national flag on their houses and helped the Germans with the dirtiest tasks. Most of them were worse than the Gestapo themselves.

After a week or so, the streets became quiet. We heard that the Germans had opened some bakeries and were selling bread. We would queue quietly the whole night to obtain one loaf of bread for the family. It often happened that after we had waited all night and finally reached the sales tables, a few Gestapo men arrived and started shouting 'Juden heraus'. We were forced to step out of line and return home without the cherished bread. Sometimes we were lucky to escape alive. Fred still visited us; he often brought some bread with him and sometimes gave me sandwiches that his mother had prepared for his lunch at work. After quite some time, the German occupation forces opened a few special shops where they distributed bread, half a loaf per family, and a few frozen potatoes. After only a few days, this too was discontinued.

The first victim in our household was my 85-year-old grandfather, a dearly beloved man who always had a good word for everyone. He was always cleanly dressed and kept his long white beard nicely groomed. He could not understand what had happened and why the Germans had come to Lwów. What did they want? he wondered. We kept him safely at home, knowing that the Germans abused bearded Jews. Whenever they caught one, they hacked his beard off, forced him to dance for them, and, at last, kicked and beat him to death. Once, Grandfather slipped out of our sight and went into the street. A young German soldier detained him, said 'Du Jude', and spat in his face. Grandfather replied, 'Du Schwein.'[7] The German struck him in the face, causing him to lose consciousness. When Grandfather came around, he didn't recognize anyone and appeared to be in a trance. Several days later, we found him lying in our garden, dead. The funeral was arranged hurriedly, and only a few people were at the cemetery because everyone was afraid to walk in the streets. We returned home depressed and our neighbors came in to pray with us. Over time, we heard of many cases in which the Germans mercilessly killed old Jews in the street, torturing them to death.

The next victim in our family was my maternal aunt, Risha, a pleasant, tall woman with four children. One of her sons had sustained a severe foot injury in a bombing attack on Lwów in 1939; he was still limping. Her husband had suffered ulcers and had died a short time earlier in agony for lack of medical care and special food that could have saved him. At this time, the Germans announced that anyone receiving financial aid from the Jewish community administration must re-register. Aunt Risha, as a widow with four children, complied with the order, as did many others. She even brought two of her children along. It was a German ruse. The Nazis rounded up all the people who had come to register and sent them to their deaths. Aunt Risha's two youngest children were left with us, hungry and poorly dressed. Not long afterwards, they were caught in the street and killed.

Two weeks into the occupation, the Germans issued a special order: every Jew must wear an armband four inches wide with a blue Star of David.[8] Then came a second order: we must hand over all fur coats in our possession, including jackets with fur collars. Violators feared the death penalty. Then they found a new way of oppressing us: the Jews were to submit an enormous 'contribution' by a certain date. This decree was immediately followed by demands for two additional contributions. We awaited the deadline in terrible fear, knowing that the leaders of the community administration[9] would be the first to be killed if the money were not handed over on time. At last, we heard that the entire sum had been collected and handed over. We thought that with this the Germans might leave us alone for a while and we might breathe easily.

Food was very scarce and almost impossible to obtain. We paid exorbitant sums for bread on the black market. We bought some wheat from a peasant and ground it in a coffee maker. The wheat was wet, and grinding it was a very difficult task that required us to work together. With the flour, we baked bread in our oven. My mother concealed several pieces of our bread under her skirt so that we should not see it and took it over to a poor family in our neighborhood that had nothing to eat. We were so hungry that once, when we saw her doing this, we took the bread and ate it ourselves.

Now we heard from my brother Adolf: he had been taken prisoner by the Germans and was in a prison camp in Helm. Adolf had been in the medical corps and refused to flee with the others during the German offensive because the Soviets had sustained many casualties on the battlefield. Imek had been with him and begged him to escape with him. Adolf refused; duty came first. After the battle, the Germans held onto the Soviet soldiers whom they had captured but released all the Ukrainians and sent them home. One of the released men had been together with Adolf, who gave him a picture of Father. On the back of the photo, he wrote that with God's help we would see each other again. I still have the picture and treasure it dearly. The Ukrainian told us that Adolf was serving as an interpreter and that his officer had promised to take him to Berlin with him. Adolf wanted some underwear, he added; somebody had stolen his last pair after he had washed it and hung it out to dry.

My parents put together a package of food and underwear and sent it to Helm with someone. By the time it arrived, Adolf was dead – killed along with all the other Jewish soldiers among the Soviet POWs.

It was a tragedy for us all, and we tried to keep it a secret from his wife Rachel, who was with us all this time. She was unable to go to her parents, who lived in the small town of Przeworsk.[10] They were poor people who had five young children. She never found out what became of them. They were probably killed in the Germans' first pogroms against the Jews.

Filip was working with a building engineer and did not wear the armband because he was tall, blond, and blue-eyed. He simply did not look like a Jew. We were able to live on his salary, even though it was not very high. One day, while repairing the roof of a tall building for the Germans, he stepped on the cover of an elevator shaft that broke under his weight. He fell from a height of three stories. As he fell, he cried out 'Father,' imagining that his father was near him. Luckily, one of the other workers heard it and called the foreman. Together with some others, they opened a brick wall, took him out, and sent him to a hospital. One of his friends brought us his bicycle and told us what had happened. We only knew that he was alive. We went to the hospital the next day and found out that he had crushed his ribs and cut his wrists, probably due to air pressure as he fell. Filip didn't stay in the hospital for long. They put gypsum bandages on his chest and discharged him. He had a very hard time at home because he could neither move about nor wash himself. The bandages were not changed for a long time. After a while, we removed them despite the lingering pain; he could not bear the dirt underneath. A short time later, although not perfectly healed, he went out to look for another job.

A brief period of uneventful life followed, except for what we heard going on in the streets – the Germans' behavior and, specifically, their brutality and abuse of Jews. Once, when our entire family was gathered in the yard among the fruit trees, the manager of the building opposite ours came over. Before the war, we had known him as a janitor. Now he managed several large buildings. He had received this fine job because he was a Ukrainian. He was visiting us this day to choose a few of us to wash the floors in his buildings. Naturally, he looked me straight in the eye and told me to go with him. I found the thought of scrubbing his floors unbearable. He insisted and threatened to call the police if I didn't go. My sister Cill begged him to leave me alone and volunteered to go instead. After lengthy hesitation, he agreed.

One day, a young Ukrainian policeman approached me in the street and ordered me to go with him. I obeyed because I knew that no *Aktion* – a round-up of a specified number of Jews for deportation to the gas chambers or to be shot in the woods – was taking place at this time. Since I was not far from home, I asked him politely to come home with me so that I could tell my parents that I was under arrest. When my father saw me, he immediately ran to a neighbor in the building next door. Another tenant in the building was an older police officer who had been a friend of my father's for many years. Father brought him to our house. When the young policeman saw the officer, he turned and fled.

For our New Year holidays, *Rosh Hashanah* and Yom Kippur,[11] all the neighbors gathered at our home for prayers. Fred and I had to stay on watch near the entrance gate lest a German or Ukrainian enter and find the entire assemblage, in which case everyone would probably be arrested. It was an awesome sight, all those people praying to God and asking for help, for a miracle... It was very difficult to keep the women quiet. Some had already lost their husbands and children. After the prayers, they went home, one by one.

Fred stayed with us for a little while and blew out the candles. He was visiting me every day at that point, but I had the feeling that this would soon come to an end. One evening, he told me that one of his friends had said he had seen his name on a list in the Gestapo office. I felt that he was afraid of being accused of collaboration with the Jews and wanted to stop seeing me. It was pointless to ask him to continue meeting or to beg him for favors, because his parents were against me. I had found this out from the mother of my friend Ada, who had once gone to Fred's house to give his mother some shirts and other clothes in exchange for some flour that Fred's father had brought home from the bakery where he worked. This kind of barter was commonplace. People, rich and poor, gave all they had. Even gems, earrings, and gold watches were exchanged for food. Be this as it may, Fred stopped seeing me with no explanation. It was a terrible shock. I couldn't adjust to the thought that he would not come anymore. Once or twice I went out to the yard nervously on days when he used to come without fail. Maybe he would come after all, I thought. I expected him and wanted to see him so much. I closed myself in my room and cried. Nobody at our home mentioned his name anymore, but I couldn't forget him. My suffering was unbearable. The Germans had imposed a 6.00 p.m. curfew, and since we were not allowed to be on the streets in the evening, his company then had meant very much to me.

Early one afternoon, a German soldier drove into our yard and asked for my father. He wanted to have the leaky radiator in his car repaired. My father brought out some tools and started to work on the car. The German drew out his pistol and ordered him to work faster because he was in a rush. Father, trembling as he soldered the radiator, told him that he had also been a soldier, a member of the Austrian forces in the First World War. The German answered him sharply that this was why Germany had lost the war. The rest of us watched them from the window and were relieved when the German left. Father came in, shaking and nervous, and said, 'What a terrible thing it is. We were together in one army then and fought for the same nation as equals, and now I have to hear this ... I left my wife and two small children by themselves without money and went to fight for them, and now I have to hear this.' How upset my father was. He had once been a very energetic man; we believed he could do anything. Everyone who came into contact with him loved him. He was now a dispirited wreck of a man. At night we sometimes heard him sighing or perhaps crying. We saved all the fruit from our trees for him, no matter how hungry we were.

Now we heard a new rumor: the Germans had ordered the closing of a certain section of Lwów,[12] the Kleparów area under the bridge, to make a ghetto for us. Some said that they were establishing concentration camps on Janowska Street.[13] At this time, my sister-in-law Klara, Imek's wife, gave birth to a girl whom we called Emma. They came to live with us. My parents loved their granddaughter dearly and bartered everything they still had at home to keep her fed. My sister-in-law traded my brother's clothes, since he was away.

Our ordinary daily menu consisted of bread, which we bought one loaf at a time. Father cut it into thin slices and doled it out equally. We even collected crumbs that were left on the table and ate them because we were still hungry. The bread tasted like the best pie we had ever dreamed of. Sometimes we also had some frozen potatoes, which Mother used to make soup. We bought the bread from a Gentile neighbor. Once the neighbor offered us a way of making some money if we wished: he would buy bread from the Gypsies, who were able to amass extra points on their ration cards by overstating the size of their families. They could always spare some rationed bread and sell it on the black market for high prices. The neighbor, a friend of my brother Filip's, talked us into taking 50 loaves to re-sell to other Jews, in the course of which we could save some loaves for ourselves. We went into the deal, even though Father was reluctant, afraid, and skeptical of the neighbor's bona fides. My brother Filip took responsibility for the matter and assured us that the whole matter must be on the up-and-up.

The neighbor brought us the bread in baskets, covered to mask its contraband nature, and we delivered it to a cousin of ours who lived across town on Peltewna Street, a neighborhood populated mostly by Jews. It was a distance of two miles, through streets full of Germans and Ukrainians who watched all passersby and often stopped them for identification. When we got there, our cousin called her neighbors, who came to buy the bread. We made a few trips with the baskets during the day and came home safely. We carried out three transactions with the neighbor and everything went well. Our profit was several loaves of bread for our family.

The fourth time, the neighbor asked us to pay for the bread in advance, claiming that he had no money of his own to give his Gypsy vendors. My father was suspicious and hesitant, but my brother again insisted on giving the money because he trusted the man. Filip himself delivered the money – 750 zloty, quite a sum under the circumstances. The bread was not delivered that evening and we suspected that something had gone wrong. Filip went over to the neighbors' house to see what had happened, but they said they had not received the money and could not get the bread anymore. We could not prove a thing and were afraid even to say a word about it. It was all the money we had; now we were broke.

Filip felt disgusted, disappointed, and guilty for having believed in the man. He could not forgive himself for what he had done to us. I forgot my hunger when I looked at the faces of my father and brother. Filip then went out to look for work, because every working person had a stamped card that allowed him to pass freely from one section of town to the other. My father also took a job at Tom's flour mill and brought my brother Max with him. In the evenings, we sat together at home and discussed politics. We read in the papers that the Germans had already moved deep into Russia. When we heard that the United States had declared war against Germany, we hoped that this would soon lead to the Nazis' demise and save our lives. People on the street even bet that we would be free within weeks.

At the entrance to Lwów,[14] where Janowska Street ended, there was a large vacant lot where the Germans had piled up quantities of lumber and building materials. Nobody knew exactly what they had in mind. People speculated that the Germans wanted to build a military camp. We could never imagine that it would become one of the most horrible places for us.

The horror began one day when German occupation officers ordered the Jewish community administration to provide them with workers to build barracks and fences on the lot. The administration, staffed by the leading Jews in Lwów, was always the address to which the Germans turned for anything they wanted. The administration had no choice but to comply. Its officials had been chosen by the Jews as their leaders. They had always been honored by both the Jews and the Poles. These people played important roles in every field of industry and commerce. Now they inducted a group of young people for the construction work, intending to replace them after a week's labor with another group. The Germans had other plans; after the first few days, they demanded more and more workers for the job. Naturally, the workers were not paid for their toil. Nor did they receive any food. At first, the community administration received a few carloads of bread and frozen potatoes for distribution to the Jews, but that was not enough for the poorest, who had nothing at all.

This went on for a few weeks. During that time, the vacant lot took on a new form. People reported that it had become a large camp with barracks and fences all around. It seemed to be a prison camp. One day, as the workers finished up and were ready to leave for home as usual, they were surrounded by SS men and were told that they would not be leaving again. From now on, this would be their home. This marked the beginning of the Janowska camp, where the German beasts would torture tens of thousands of people to death.

3 The Italians

Meanwhile, we learned that the Germans had brought Italian soldiers[15] into Lwów and headquartered them at the palace of Duke Szeptycki on Zielona Street, a spacious building with many rooms and a fenced yard. There the Italians established their offices and the mess and dining halls for their enlisted men and officers. Hearing that they needed workers, my sister Cill and I went there to apply. We found a few maintenance workers on the premises – people whom we had known before the war as wealthy merchants and senior officials. They had never done maintenance work before and were not being paid for it now; they had volunteered for it because it entitled them to a stamped card that spared them from being sent to the Janowska camp.

We joined them. Our job was to clean the place. My sister Cill tired of it very quickly, not because of the work itself – there was little to do and there were many girls to do it – but because of the type of work. She and several other girls left after a few days. I stayed on, along with a girl named Kama and two sisters, Rogia and Sara.

Meanwhile, my brother Filip was still looking for a job on the 'Aryan'[16] side of the town, as we called the area where only Christians lived. One day he met a construction worker at a restaurant and spoke with him about a job. As Filip spoke, he took out his handkerchief and his armband slipped out with it. Two Ukrainian police arrested him on the spot, stripped him of his overcoat and wristwatch, and escorted him on a streetcar to the Janowska camp. One of our neighbors saw him in the streetcar and came to tell us the bad news. It was a terrible shock to us; my parents could hardly overcome it.

Filip was the only member of our household who earned money for his work, since his looks made it possible for him to work in the non-Jewish part of town.

At first we were able to send him small food parcels through the community administration, which collected such parcels and forwarded them to prisoners at Janowska. However, this practice was soon discontinued. The parcels were distributed to the inmates while they were assembled together, and as one man's name was called out, hundreds of other hungry prisoners would grab the parcel and tear it to pieces for the food it contained. When this happened, the Germans shot at the people. One day they killed several prisoners in this fashion and wounded others, including Filip. He was shot in the leg and could hardly walk, but a friend supported him when they went to and from work in the stone quarries to which they had been assigned. The Germans killed others who had been more seriously injured; they had no use for people who could not work.

The people who gave Father this information advised him to use all his influence with the community administration to have Filip taken to a hospital. Otherwise, he would be killed. Father had to donate 15 beds to the hospital in the Jewish section. He bought them with the last money that we could collect. My sister Cill sold her furniture and handed over the proceeds. With this, we moved Filip to the hospital.

Just then, another group of Italians moved into the palace where I worked and opened a special officers' mess and another dining hall. One of the newly arrived soldiers was Roberto, a short, dark-skinned fellow with green eyes. He was about 22 years of age. He spoke a little bit of German and was in charge of the food stores. The girls surrounded him because they wanted him to hire them for the mess. This was our dream, for there we could at least get something to eat. The girls showered him with compliments and promised him fine gifts if he hired them. I stood aside helplessly amidst all this because I had nothing to offer him. Somehow, he saw me standing there, came over to me, and asked how old I was.

'Thirty,' I answered. 'And how old are you?'

He smiled at me and answered, 'Seventy.'

After that, all the girls took their handbags and left for their homes. I could not find my handbag and I hunted around for it. At last, he called me over and gave it to me.

The next day, as the girls and I were being transferred to another building, Roberto called me over and invited me to come work in the sergeants' mess. The menu that day – I still remember it – was macaroni with sausages. It was my job to serve the tables in the mess hall. On the way there, our people stood still and begged me with their eyes for some food. I carried the dishes a short distance only and could not give them anything. They were terribly angry at me and accused me of being stubborn. At last, I went back to the kitchen, not noticing that somebody had spilled water from the macaroni on the floor. I slipped and fell, drenching myself. I was terribly scared that Roberto would fire me for being so clumsy. Instead of scolding me, however, he told me to dry my clothes near the fireplace and said he would take in the dishes. 'Don't worry,' he added, promising to take care of me because he liked me.

The next day, we returned to the palace, where an officers' mess had been opened. The place was specially decorated because generals ate there; even Mussolini's daughter had once attended a special dinner there. On my first day of work in this facility, I had to light the fire in the stove. It being the first time in my life that I had to do this, I could hardly manage it. One of the officers who passed by watched me and asked me who I was. I was wearing a white silk blouse. It amazed him to find a girl looking like that working there. Just then, Roberto came in and explained to the officer that I was Jewish and that Jews had to work there without pay. The officer had never heard of this before; in fact, he did not know what was going on in the place. He gave me a pitying look, walked out, returned a moment later, gave me a box of candies, and ordered another soldier to fire up the stove. On top of that, I received the food that remained in the kitchen before I went home in the afternoon.

I was very happy that day and told everyone at home about my new job. They were pleased with my good fortune, and Mother asked me to retell the story of how I had been chosen over all the others for this assignment, despite my fears. Now I thought that apart from receiving food for myself I might even be able to bring some home.

Two other girls were hired at this time. One was Miriam, 22 years old. She was married; her husband was in the Soviet army and she knew nothing of his whereabouts. The other was Henrietta. Roberto was still in charge of the food stores, but he had an additional assignment: supervising the cooks. Two men, Luciano and Sabattini, did the cooking. Luciano, from Milan, was a harsh and vulgar man who tended to be sour with everyone. Sometimes he even quarreled with Roberto for no reason. Sabattini was a peasant from a village near Rome. Married and about 25 years old, he was a man of good character. He understood our plight and took care of me and Miriam especially.

Once, Roberto sent me to his bedroom to clean it, although he knew it was clean. The moment I entered, he moved in behind me and tried to embrace me. Just then, Sabattini appeared at the door. He knew Roberto too well and understood what he meant by sending me to his bedroom. The actual cleaning, he knew, was always done by an older woman. He therefore followed Roberto whenever he heard him instruct me to go there, or to the cellar for coals, or to any other place. Sabattini could be my older brother, I felt.

On two occasions, the Germans conducted *Aktionen* in which they rounded up all Jews whom they found in the street and sent them to their deaths. Both times, the Italians kept Miriam and me with them. When they heard what was going on outside, they ordered us to sleep in the food storeroom that night and didn't let us go home. Our hearts pounded like drums all night long, in fear for ourselves and for our families at home. Would we see them tomorrow when we got back? The next day, Roberto told me that he had spent the entire night sleeping on an easy chair near the door of the storeroom, lest anything happen to us.

One day, Luciano sent me to the bathroom for some butter, which was kept on blocks of ice in the bathtub along with other perishable foods. The moment I leaned into the tub to pick up the butter, Luciano seized me from behind and tried to kiss me. This time, Roberto had followed the would-be assailant. There he was at the entrance to the bathroom, hands in his pockets, shouting at Luciano, 'Let her go!' Luciano and Roberto always fought over something, and this time it was me. Whenever Luciano could, he gave me the hardest chores, such as chopping meat for hamburgers for all those officers. It was a hard job indeed, and I was weak by then. Roberto always came to my rescue, even though as the storeroom manager he didn't have to work in the kitchen.

Once they gave me a nice white apron and ordered me to carry a large tray with cocktail glasses into the mess. As I opened the door, all the officers turned to look at me. I became dizzy and unwittingly struck the door jamb with the tray. Several glasses tipped over, fell to the floor, and shattered. I nearly fainted. In a split second, Roberto moved to my side, held me in his arms, told me he would pay for the damage if necessary, and assured me that I need not fear on that account. The captain in charge of the mess then brought me a glass of brandy and told me to forget about the whole thing.

We felt good during those weeks. We had food, a place to work, and safety. We were better off than the others, who were with the Germans. Luciano hated Roberto and could not stand to be near him. He tried to convince me that Roberto was from Sicily; in other words, that he was a lowlife. Back there, Luciano said, Roberto was a different kind of guy. He was faking the role of a cultured man by putting on sunglasses and carrying a camera. Roberto was very stubborn, Luciano continued, and had easy money that he made in illegal ways. Seeing Roberto's sincere wish to help me, I didn't believe a word of it.

Whenever high-ranking officers visited headquarters, we had to stay at work until late and were driven home in our bosses' cars, usually by Roberto and a chauffeur. One could feel the emptiness in the streets. Only some German soldiers on patrol could be seen. Curfew went into effect at 8.00 p.m. The Germans were so strict in carrying out the curfew orders that they shot at anything that moved, even a shadow. On one occasion when Roberto brought me home late, my father came out to thank him and asked Roberto to take good care of me because I was still a naïve young girl. Roberto solemnly promised to do so.

My father still worked in Tom's flour mill, where he had worked during the Soviet occupation. Every worker had a stamped card that entitled him to go to and from work freely and to have a woman to do his housekeeping and cooking. This meant that my mother was allowed to remain at home. Imek's wife Klara held a job and my sister Hela stayed home to take care of Klara's child because she was on Klara's card. However, Cill and Rachel, Adolf's wife, had no cards and we feared for their safety. Imek and Klara's daughter was very sweet. My parents loved her dearly; she was the only source of fun in their lives.

Just then, Roberto's attitude toward me changed. Now he was very mean to me at times. Once, when all the others went home after work, I stood around talking with Rutka, a girl who had just come to work with us. Roberto came by and ordered me to return to work. I tried to explain that it would then be too late for me to go home and that everything in the kitchen was clean and in good order. Stubbornly he insisted that I return to work. Just as I gave up and headed back to the kitchen, he changed his mind and told me to go home because he could do nothing with me. I responded to his advances as frigidly as a log; never did I repay him for every-thing he did for me.

Filip was in the hospital, his leg healing. However, the doctors had not set the bones well and they knit in the wrong position. We wanted to spend as much time as possible at the hospital because there we could at least see him and give him something from time to time. Roberto gave me bread and my brother sometimes provided sweets. Filip was always happy to see me and greeted me with a hearty kiss each time. My parents and I would sit near him and put on happy faces. Inside, however, we were so afraid and worried that we could hardly speak. We saw others lying in their beds, poor and hungry, without sufficient medical care and drugs. The doctors visited them but had no remedies to offer. One of the patients approached me and asked for a piece of bread. Another asked me to bring him potato peelings; those would suffice, he said. It was horrible to be among these people. Some of the patients were very lonely. Their families had been killed, and with no one to visit them and bring them essentials, they simply died slowly of hunger.

4 *The August* Aktion

Not all the forced laborers carried those specially stamped cards.[17] All the undocumented workers were taken away in August, when the largest and most horrible *Aktion* in Lwów began. In that *Aktion*, the Germans rounded up 30,000 people and sent them to their deaths. Everyone with a stamped card was allowed to go to work as usual. Since we were among the documented, we expected to be spared this time around. The *Aktion* lasted for three weeks. We thought it would never end. On the first night of the *Aktion*, we didn't go home from work. Our bosses gave us some blankets and sent us to the attic, where we settled for the night. The next day, they told us that we were safe because we had stamped cards and we could go home. Roberto accompanied us home, promised that nothing adverse would happen to us, and tried to convince us that we had nothing to fear.

My parents thought I would be much safer at home than at work. Our house had a large cellar that one entered through a trap door in the kitchen. The cellar became our hide-out. My two sisters, Hela and Cill, my sister-in-law Rachel, and some of our neighbors and their children spent long periods of time there. To avert suspicion, a kitchen cabinet was placed over the trap door and a bench and a pail of laundry were stationed nearby. The fugitives down below had to maintain silence, every move they heard in the kitchen overhead filled them with terror. Nobody knew how long this would last. Three policemen – usually one German, one Ukrainian, and one from the Jewish police – came by to search all the houses for potential hiding places and then to inspect the occupants' cards. Half an hour later, another group of three policemen visited to repeat the process. Our anxiety spiked each time anew.

The first night that I spent in this fashion passed quietly. Early the following morning, I went to work as usual. I felt safe there and believed that my stamped card would protect me. On the way I met Henrietta, one of my co-workers at this time – Maria and Ruth were the others – and we went on together. Policemen checked our cards on every street corner. We advanced from one inspection to the next, frightened for a moment and then happy to get our cards back. The way seemed longer than ever before. We thought it might never end. The streets were empty; even Christians were afraid to be outside. From time to time, streetcars passed by with trailers crowded with men, women, and children. We saw their scared faces and heard them crying. At the corners of the cars were members of the Gestapo wearing steel helmets and ready to fire at anyone who tried to move. We went on our way, our hearts pounding like drums, afraid of everyone who looked at us.

From far away we saw an SS man waving at us and calling us to come to him. Although he was standing on a street corner that was not on our way, we saw no choice but to obey; otherwise he might shoot us. We thought we were done for. The SS man was a tall, skinny fellow with the look of a tiger. Near him stood a Ukrainian policeman and a Gestapo soldier. He confiscated our cards and ordered us to enter the building on the corner and go upstairs. 'Die Karten sind gestampelt,' I explained. In response, he tore our cards to pieces, struck me across the face, and told us again to go upstairs. Ukrainians stood on the stairs, pounding each person who passed, especially men whom they had caught on the streets. When we entered the room at the top of the stairs, we saw a spectacle that stopped our hearts and froze the blood in our veins. The room was filled with men who had been beaten, their faces torn, their heads marred by open wounds, blood streaming down their bodies, arms broken. Some women were there, too, their eyes expressing their terror. The windows were shut; nobody was allowed to approach them. We had to stay next to each other, men on one side and women on the other, separated by the Ukrainians.

It was a hot day. I was wearing a white woolen sweater and I felt myself perspiring. I could hardly breathe and I thought I would suffocate. The air was so thick that you could cut it with a knife. At last, they opened a small window. Henrietta moved toward the window. Although a policeman struck her twice with a club, she managed somehow to write a few words on a scrap of paper: 'Help us. The Germans have caught us.' She addressed the message to the Italians' headquarters and threw the note out the window. I stood in front of her to conceal her action from prying eyes. When it was over, I told her that it was nonsensical. Nobody would notice this scrap of paper except, maybe, the Gestapo, since nobody else was on the street at the time.

Meanwhile, the SS man who had arrested us entered the room along with a pretty girl, a tall blonde who seemed to be 17 years of age. She had been beaten on her way to the room, and the SS man decided to finish her off in our presence. He hit her several times with a whip, and when she fell to the floor unconscious he kicked her with his heavy boots. When it was over, he ordered a policeman to carry her out. Then he waved his whip in our direction, saying that he had caught the girl without an armband and that all of us were going to die. He himself had killed 13,000 people, he bragged, and now 30,000 were going to be killed. His face and eyes were the monstrous organs of a bloodthirsty beast.

In the afternoon, German trucks came to deliver us to the German Kommissariat (headquarters) on Kazimierzowska Street. There we met hundreds of others who had been captured; they were waiting in a spacious, fenced-in yard that was heavily guarded by the Gestapo. By chance, a German soldier came by just then to look for a certain girl who worked with him. The girl ran toward him joyfully, but a Gestapo man who was nearby struck her and pushed her back. Then, shouting and cursing, he ordered the soldier to leave the place immediately. The German lowered his eyes in shame and went away.

Several hours later, a high-ranking German officer entered the yard and ordered everyone with a stamped card to step out. A few people still had their cards; they moved forward. Henrietta and I did not have our cards because the SS man had shredded them. The Germans in the yard would never believe this, we knew, because we had no right to say anything about this SS man. At this point, trucks drove in to deliver us to a new destination: the Janowska camp. We were packed like sardines and could hardly move our limbs. Right near me stood a German guard, a young Gestapo soldier.

'How old are you?' he asked me.

'Seventeen,' I replied.

'You're very young, but you can't help it. You're all going to die, perhaps even today.'

This was impossible, I told him. 'The German Wehrmacht won't do this to us. We've done nothing wrong.'

He nodded, smiling. 'We will see.'

We passed our house as we moved down Janowska Street. People who lived nearby stood outside, observing the crowded cars. Noticing our Christian neighbors among them, I buried myself inside the car. I did not want to be seen by them lest they tell my parents, whom I wished to keep in the dark.

The Janowska camp was on a large field enclosed by an electrified fence marked with a skull and crossbones. Some distance ahead, we saw guard turrets and heard shooting from time to time. Farther inside were barracks. We were deposited in the field, in the burning sun, without food or water. Sobbing and sighing were heard from every direction. Small children were crying. An elderly woman near us had been shot in the arm; her blood streamed over her hand and onto her clothes. Her daughter sat next to her, patting her mother's arm and crying together with her. I encountered some of our neighbors, including an older woman and two young girls who had worked for Italian officers in their homes. We shared each other's stories, describing where we had worked and how we had been arrested. We became friends very quickly and even borrowed each other's comb, mirror, and lipstick.

We sat on the grass, frightened. Nobody was allowed to get up. Those who disobeyed were immediately shot by the Gestapo guard in the turret. I put a little girl on my knees and tried to stop her from crying by telling her fairy tales. She cried anyway; she had lost her mother somewhere in the crowd. Henrietta saw relatives who she had been sure were safely hidden in a cellar in the Italian headquarters building. Nobody had known about the place, she figured; it was in a safe part of town. The janitor of the building had been paid a lot of money for that hiding place and had promised to keep them safe there. Within a few hours, the field was crowded with people who had been brought in from town.

Gestapo men milled among us, ordering us to give them wristwatches, rings, earrings, fountain pens, and other valuables. They filled boxes with these items. Heartsick and fearful, the people coughed up whatever they had. Some tried to hide a few things or hesitated to give away objects of sentimental value. The Gestapo men shot them on the spot. An elderly woman sitting near me dug a hole in the ground and placed a valuable ring there, hoping to come back later and remove it. After the Germans collected everything, they ordered us to line up four abreast. We formed long rows and waited like this for hours. I thought it would never end. Not having eaten all day, I was very weak and hungry. Then I looked around and felt better. At least I did not see anyone else from my family.

In the midst of my reverie, I heard a voice calling, 'Die Jenigen die bei der Italienischen Wehrmacht arbeiteten heraus!' (All those working for the Italian Wehrmacht, step out!) I was too deep in thought to realize that this meant me. A woman standing near me pushed me out of the ranks and told me to run over. As I pushed my way through, another woman asked me to take her children along. Others asked me to contact their families outside. I was too faint to understand a word of it. When I reached the appointed place, I saw a German officer and the Italian soldier who had come for us, an Alpinist who wore a special hat with a feather and spoke fluent German. Meanwhile, Henrietta and other girls approached the officer. One of the Gestapo men asked me for my labor permit. I did not have it, I answered, because it had been taken away from me that morning. The Italian interrupted and said, 'This is our Klara. She works in the officers' mess and I know her very well.' There were nine girls in all. Five of them had never worked with us but were smart enough to seize the moment and join us. Since the Italian soldier did not know the rest of them, he asked me whether they all worked there. Yes, I said. With that, the Italian soldier escorted us out of the camp.

Another Italian soldier, on a motorcycle at the gate, was sent back to headquarters immediately to notify them that we were free and on our way back to work. We went down Janowska Street. When we passed my house, I asked for permission to stop for a moment and visit my mother. My mother was standing at the door, wondering when she saw me enter the yard what I was doing there during the day, when I was supposed to be at work. I rushed to her, kissed her, and described briefly what had happened. 'I'm back, Mother. The Italians came to save me and are waiting for me to return with them. I have to go now ... Don't worry, Mother, I'll probably sleep there until things quiet down again. Meanwhile, goodbye.' I saw tears in Mother's eyes as she kissed me and escorted me to the waiting group.

As we drove away, she stood there for a long time and waved. How pretty she was, I thought – tall, slim, with dark eyes and black, curly hair. She was wearing one of the dresses that she had handmade for me; it fit her now. I looked back at her and waved until we lost sight of each other. On our way, we passed several groups of Jews who were being led by German police to the Janowska camp.

Halfway to Italian headquarters, we rendezvoused with a

military car that had been sent out to pick us up. When the car stopped, Roberto jumped out, ran toward me, hoisted me in his strong arms, and placed me in the car. I could see the joy in his eyes. Our rescue had been his doing, I realized. On the way back to headquarters, he sat near me and explained how the Italians had received the slip of paper that Henrietta threw out the window. An anonymous person simply handed it to them and disappeared. Their officer told them to do what they could to find us and bring us back. They immediately sent their people in several directions to look for us. They checked every police post until they came to the Janowska camp. To this day, I do not know the identity of the man who picked up the note and gave it to the Italians, thus saving nine people's lives. He must have had lots of courage and a big heart. Most people were afraid to be anywhere near where Jews were being arrested. In such cases, the Germans arrested everyone in sight, and any Christian among the detainees had to go to a lot of trouble to prove his identity.

When we arrived at the mess hall, all the officers came to see us. The soldiers were so glad to have us back that they personally served us food and drinks. The officers asked us how it had happened, but we could hardly understand them because we were not yet fluent in Italian. After the officers left, the soldiers climbed to the attic and laid out bags of straw as bedding for us. Some of the girls worked for officers in their homes; they were driven away in the officers' cars. The others went home.

Meanwhile, the *Aktion* continued. We heard and saw the Germans 'cleansing' street after street. Early one morning, we learned that Rutka's mother and brother had been arrested. Thus, pretty, 16-year-old Rutka was left alone with her invalid twin sister, who had suffered polio as a child and had legs of different lengths. Rutka was very friendly with me and this earned me the enmity of one of the older officers, a colonel. Once this officer asked Rutka to come to his apartment, clean the place for him, and take a bath there. I advised Rutka not to go and explained that she would be better off with us in the kitchen than working for him. She was too young to have an affair, I said. Rutka's brother – a tall, delicate young student – also worked with us. His job was to clean and polish the floors. Whenever meals were served, he stood in the hallway and waited for his food until the cooks and waiters had finished eating. Rutka and her sister stayed with us. Her sister was very depressed and always sat in a corner.

Through the windows, we saw people being led away by the Germans: young and old, crying children, all miserable. Some carried small bundles with their belongings, hoping to use them in new places of residence or hard labor. Once, as we looked on dejectedly, one of the Italian soldiers – a slim, dark fellow named Bruno – came over and told us that everyone in the building across from ours was dead. A friend of mine named Sara and her family had lived there. Bruno used to visit the building sometimes and bring them some food. The last time he did so, he entered the first room and saw a stream of blood on the floor. Opening the next door, he saw the whole family lying on the floor, their throats cut and the room flooded with their blood. As I sank into depression over the horror of their collective suicide, Roberto stepped in and told me that I had a telephone call.

It was my sister Cill. In a tearful and pleading voice, she begged for help. Everyone in our house had been taken away except for Cill, who had managed to run away and go into hiding. She couldn't be on the streets. The police would come in two groups, she related. One group would step out of the house while the other entered to search for Jews. There was a Jewish policeman in the party; it was his duty to pursue and capture escapees, whom the Germans then finished off in their barbaric way. All I remember of my response to this ghastly information was falling against the wall, striking my head, and fainting. As I fell, Roberto grabbed the receiver and continued to talk to my sister. Then he went out to meet her and brought her over to us. Cill sat with me on the stairs in back of the kitchen and we cried. She told me that they had taken Mother, our sister Hela, Rachel, and the baby, who was eight months old. Imek's wife, Klara, had the good fortune of being at work. Neighbors who had no cards and were hiding in our cellar were also taken.

My mother paid for her kindness in hiding our neighbors. Since she had a stamped card, she had not been hiding and kept the baby with her in the kitchen. The entrance to the cellar had been camouflaged, and Mother had put a crib near the cupboard over the trap door. As the search proceeded, the soldiers came and went, checked my mother's card repeatedly, and then stepped out. A group of soldiers who had visited the house in the morning came back. A Gestapo man with them ordered Mother to tell him where the people were hiding. One of our neighbors must have denounced her. Mother, shivering, did not answer him. The Gestapo man stepped into the yard and returned with our dog. He thought the dog would bark at the spot where he smelled the people hiding, but the animal remained silent. Then the Gestapo man pulled out a bayonet and dropped it on the floor here and there. A hollow sound gave away the location of the trap door. He pushed the cupboard aside, opened the trap door, and ordered all the people to climb out. They obeyed, pale and trembling with fear. They were counted – some of them were whole families – and pushed out. Cill asked a Ukrainian policeman for permission to get her armband from a closet in her bedroom. Once inside, she stepped into a closet, buried herself in the hanging clothes, and closed the door from the inside. The Ukrainian went in to look for her, did not see her, and left the house together with the others. When the coast was clear, Cill ran into a post office and telephoned me.

Cill told me all this while sitting with me on the stairs. Poor Mother had to leave her home clutching the baby, a poor little creature who didn't understand where she was being taken. They were all led somewhere to be burned. On the way, they were beaten. Mother was beaten especially badly for having concealed the fugitives. Jews in Lwów hid in all kinds of places, believing that they would not be found. In some cases, people hid in a baker's oven. Once, during a search, a man slipped into a barrel that stood unnoticed in the yard.

I received only one message from my mother and sister. A Gentile who worked nearby visited the kitchen one day and said that Hela had given him my address at work and asked him to tell me that they needed some bread, if I could spare any. I went to Sabattini and asked him for some. He gave it to me but with a pitying gesture, as if to say that they would never need it. The man took the bread and went away. I do not know if the bread ever reached its destination. Its intended recipients were carried away in sealed wagons just like animals. They were packed tightly with no air to breathe. Those who tried to leap from the slow-moving train were shot.

Cill and I stayed at the Italian headquarters and worked together for a while. When Roberto was transferred to another mess several blocks away, he took Cill to his new place, a much larger and busier facility that served all ranks up to sergeant. A few days later, we decided to go home in the afternoon to visit our father and our brother Max. The *Aktion* was still in progress, but now they were taking only men to the camp. We obtained a loaf of bread and left for home. We found Father and Max in a severely depressed and foul mood. When they saw us enter, they fell into our arms and the four of us cried. Father was in bad shape and had aged terribly. He told us that the evening they took Mother away, he had come home and found a pot of buckwheat groats on the kitchen stove, completely burned. Mother had been cooking them for supper. The house had been ransacked; the closets were empty. The perpetrators, we figured, were bands of youths who followed the police, entered houses after they had left, and looted the buildings of everything they could carry. The Gestapo men had returned that evening, Father said, in the company of Wladek Ulman, a neighbor who used to work for us and had learned a trade in our shop. He led the Gestapo directly to the cellar. One of the Gestapo agents drew a handgun, pointed it at my father's heart, and asked him where all the people who had been hiding there had gone. The Gestapo had taken them all, Father replied. In response, the soldier shouted, 'If you lie to us, I'll shoot you like a dog.' They reeked of alcohol and were obviously drunk.

After they left, Filip came home. He had been unshaven for a long time and was wearing torn, dirty clothes. He told Father that the police had come into the hospital, loaded all the patients onto trucks, and hauled them away. He had managed to jump out a window and come home. Father, sobbing, pleaded with him to go into hiding somewhere. He did not want to see the Germans shoot Filip when they found him here. Filip left for parts unknown.

The bread we had brought with us was untouched. We were in such agony that we thought we would never be able to eat anything again.

At work the next day, I knew I had to pass the time and went about my duties like an automaton. Around noon, Sabattini came over and told me that someone near the fence was asking for me. Sabattini had tried to get rid of him, but he had insisted. When I walked to the fence, I faced someone whom I hardly recognized – a wretch with a long beard and a twisted leg. It was Filip. I could not stop crying. I found a hole in the fence and led him in through the back of the yard. We sat on the grass and he told me that he had spent the past three days and nights in the attic of a house occupied by German soldiers. He knew the place well because he had once worked there and managed to enter unnoticed. His sole nourishment during that time was rainwater that he had found in a barrel. I told him to wait for me. I went to the dining room, gathered leftover macaroni from the tables, wrapped it in paper, and brought it to Filip. He ate quietly and consumed everything in a matter of minutes.

Then I asked Sabattini for money with which Filip could go to a barber for a shave. It was a risk that he had to take; he could not circulate in this state. Soon Filip returned, clean-shaven. He even refunded the money, the barber having refused payment for the shave. Sabattini told him to keep the money; he might need it for something else. Filip left and promised to be home in the evening.

It was the last day of the *Aktion*, but we did not survive it without misfortune. This time, it was my youngest brother, Max. As he and Father were coming home from work, Gestapo soldiers stopped them for an inspection, arrested Max, and took him to the Janowska camp. That evening, the four of us who remained – Father, Filip, Cill, and myself – sat together at home in a bleak frame of mind, exchanging rumors. One version had it that the entire population of the camp would be transported to death somewhere. Others said that they would be taken away for forced labor. We did not know what to believe in any case, and we still hoped to see them back home.

5 The Ghetto

During the next few days it was quieter and safer to walk on the street. People hurried to work. The Gestapo seemed to be less rude and people felt more at ease. Filip found a job as 'one of us' and did not remove his armband. Three days later, we heard that Max was working outside the Janowska camp. Inmates of the camp went to and from the camp in groups of four, guarded by Soviet prisoners armed with wooden sticks and overseen by German soldiers. They worked behind Zieleona Gora (Green Hills), not far from my workplace. When we left for work in the morning, we took a small food parcel with us and waited near the camp until Max marched out with the others. Then I walked over and handed him the package. It was a very dangerous maneuver; if the guards noticed us, they would have shot us on the spot. Max was afraid but we wanted to help him somehow. He was very young then, a sweet, boyish kid.

One day, we decided to help him escape. We went to his workplace, where he and others crushed large stones with sledgehammers for a road that was being built. The wretched workers were so tired and hungry that they could hardly lift the heavy hammers. The Soviet prisoners mingled among the workers and struck them with their sticks whenever they paused for a moment's rest. Cill and I hid behind a nearby house, took off our armbands, and waited until the prisoner in charge passed by. When he was far away, we motioned to Max to come over. Then the three of us ran to the hills and took a side path to the building where Roberto and Cill worked. The janitor of the building, a woman, allowed Max to stay in her apartment. During the day, Cill brought him food and took care of him. In the evening, I went there and took him home. That night, five of us were together.

Max was a bright kid who could always make snap decisions that proved correct. This quality now helped save his life. When he was arrested, he had given a false name and address and was duly registered that way. He had kept his work card and hid it, thinking that he might be able to use it somehow. Now that he was home again, he went to work with my father at the flour mill as if nothing had happened.

Then came another heartache. One morning we noticed that the fence around our yard, which was made of boards, was torn in several places. Our neighbors had been ripping away the boards for use in their stoves. There was nothing we could do about it. We were using our furniture as fuel so as to keep the fence around the house. The first time Father had to break a chair for firewood, his conscience would not let him do it. He had lived with this furniture for so many years that destroying it meant destroying part of his life. Now, another piece of his property, the fence, was being demolished by hooligans and he had to see it and keep quiet. We felt the same way but were equally helpless.

Soon after the August *Aktion*,[18] the Germans ordered all Jews in town to move to the Zamarstynów and Kleparów areas by a certain date. The designated areas were a slum quarter on the outskirts of Lwów, across the bridge. The people who lived there had stables and shacks where they kept horses and cows in normal times; by now, people from town were using even these hovels as living quarters. The bridge was guarded day and night by the Gestapo, who checked everything people took with them from their former homes. One never knew exactly when one could cross the bridge without being arrested. On some days, old people were stopped and arrested while crossing the bridge, even though they were together with their families and children. On other days, only women were stopped and men were allowed to cross with their belongings. Sometimes a few people were taken at random and the others passed uneventfully. There were also a few days when, incredibly, the Gestapo guards stood aside and let people go by without so much as a glance.

One day, a woman who lived in our neighborhood was stopped and arrested near the bridge. She used to come to us on Saturdays for prayers and would cry very loudly while praying. Her husband had been killed on one of the first days of the German occupation, leaving her with three small children. She had found an apartment on the other side of the bridge and went back to her former home to collect her children and some of her belongings. As she approached the bridge, a Gestapo man ordered her to cross to the other side of a wall and stay together with a large number of other women, old and young. All were facing the wall; none was allowed to turn away. Next to them was a group of men, who were subsequently taken to the Janowska camp. I met one of these men later; he told me that the woman had cried that she had left three small children without anyone to take care of them. Then and there, the Gestapo men opened fire at the women with a machine gun. No one was left alive. The men standing nearby had to watch. Some of them had wives, daughters, or mothers against the wall. These men were forced to witness the barbaric murder of their loved ones.

Cill was the first of us to go to the new Jewish ghetto across the bridge, and she found an apartment for us. We waited for her at home all that day, worried and anxious until we saw her back again. Then we rented a cart with a horse and loaded the belongings that remained in the house. We were one of the last families to cross over. Although it was a quiet day at the bridge, my heart pounded like a drum. One could never be sure what the next moment would bring and what changes might occur in the guards' minds. As I approached the bridge, I prayed that the way would be longer, because I dreaded the moment of crossing. When we crossed the bridge, I was afraid to look back at the police and Gestapo. Only after we were far from them did I breathe easily.

Cill had found us a one-story house that we were to share

with two young girls whose parents and entire family had been killed by the Germans. We moved into a large room and left the smaller room for the girls. We lit a fire in the kitchen stove with pieces of wood that the previous tenants had left behind. When that ran out, we burned our last pieces of furniture. Inmates from the Janowska camp were building a tall fence around the ghetto. I hoped they would never finish it.

Cill continued to work with Roberto in the mess. One of her colleagues was Tama, who had bought false papers in the name of a Christian girl from someone who had connections with Gentiles outside the ghetto. These Gentiles peddled documents of people who had died, such as birth certificates, work cards, and I.D. cards, and sometimes even produced bogus documents that they sold as the real thing. It was probably a family business. They would buy these documents on the cheap and sell them for very high prices. Some Gentiles sold their own documents, reported them to the police as lost, and then received new ones. Despite having such papers, Tama lived in the ghetto. Once I asked her, 'Why don't you leave the ghetto and live on the other side? You might save yourself that way. Now that you have papers certifying you as a Christian, try to get a job somewhere. You'll get paid for your work and make a living until all this is over.' We discussed it all the way home. Near her house, she invited me to come in and said, 'You'll see for yourself.'

Her apartment was a one-room affair with a small kitchen that she shared with her parents and her two-year-old daughter. The room was full of furniture and they hung washing pails and other utensils on the walls because there was no room for them anywhere else. I could hardly find a place to sit. Tama introduced me to her parents and daughter, a sweet girl with curly blond hair and blue eyes. She sat on her grandmother's knees and smiled innocently at me. I had not known about her at all. 'You see, Klara,' Tama explained, 'this is my daughter. When I was 18, I met a Russian pianist who played in a theater. He was poor when he came over here from Russia and had shabby clothes, but he seemed to be a good fellow and I liked him. My parents were against him. We went to the Sax office, signed some papers, and had our internal passports stamped. That was our wedding. When my parents found out, they felt sorry for me. I was their only daughter and they accepted it as a fait accompli. They rented a luxurious apartment for us in a new building and bought me expensive furniture. A little later, I gave birth to my daughter. We were happy then.' She sighed deeply and I saw the sadness in her eyes. Then she continued. 'Our happiness didn't last long. When the German–Russian war started and the Germans occupied our town, my husband thought we should put a nameplate with his Ukrainian name on the door. We'd be safer that way. Soon afterwards, he came home and I saw a Ukrainian emblem on his coat lapel and a ribbon with the blue and green colors of the nationalists. After that, he sometimes failed to come home at night. Then he came home only once or twice a week.

'The instant the Germans ordered us to enter the ghetto, he came home and said he would stay there and I would have to move to the ghetto and live there with my parents and daughter. Only then did I realize that my parents had been right to oppose our marriage. I hadn't understood them before. I thought they were old-fashioned and unable to understand young people. Now, I saw his poor character and how cruel he really was. I didn't mind for myself. I thought about my innocent daughter. He was her father. Not only didn't he try to help, but he sent us away.

'After a couple of months, I decided to go and see him even though I knew that I'd disgrace myself by doing so. I wanted to ask him to take the girl under his care. I left the ghetto with the child in my arms. On the way, I stepped into a hallway and took off my armband. Then I headed for my former apartment, where he now lived. A girl opened the door for me. She realized who I was and I entered the room. He was lying on the bed and didn't get up to greet me. He didn't even ask me to have a seat. I looked around at everything that my parents had bought for me, and now I had to stand there like a beggar who had no right to any of it. I asked him to take our daughter. Otherwise, her life would be in danger; she'd be taken by the Germans and killed. I myself would try to leave the ghetto and find a job to support myself.

'His girlfriend replied that she was an actress and had no time to take care of the child. He didn't say a word. I was too shocked to say a thing. I left the room with tears in my eyes that I tried to hide from them. Now I don't know how to help myself. I have to find a place for my daughter; then I'll think about myself.'

Her story reminded me of my boyfriend, Fred. I remembered when we had walked together and discussed the rumors that were circulating. The Jews would be sent to a ghetto. We would have to part. He would not be allowed to see me. I would not be able to go out. Fred took my hand and promised me that he would do everything possible to see me and help me.

My heart contracted in pain. I understood Tama's situation: to be in love, to disregard all obstacles, and then to face such disappointment. These thoughts troubled me for days. I couldn't understand how human beings could change into beasts or, worse still, how circumstances could change people. I gave Tama a brief account of my past and what I was suffering at this time. Tama accompanied me home and told me about her plans for the future. She intended to ask someone to take care of her child and then she would leave the ghetto alone.

When I came home, I found the two girls who lived with us packing their belongings. They had been ordered to move to the workplace, on the railway. They had to sleep there, too. We were sorry to part because we had become used to them and thought of them as part of our family. Now we had the apartment to ourselves.

That evening, Cill had cooked potato soup. As we sat around the table eating our supper, we heard a knock at the door. A very distinguished-looking, well-dressed, middle-aged man came into the room. Our father invited him to sit with us at the table and share our food. The man seated himself at a corner of the table. Our father placed a bowl of potato soup in front of him, and he consumed it eagerly. He was obviously very grateful. He thanked us over and over again. After supper, Father asked the guest about his family, whom, it turned out, he knew very well. Later that night, the man left. As he closed the door behind him, Father explained that he was a member of the Tom family. 'He is one of the last owners of the flour mill where I've been working.' Kaiser Franz Josef of Austria, Father continued, had once visited Lwów and honored the Toms by being their guest during his stay. They had been the wealthiest family in town.

I thought of that family's past. I used to pass their house every day. It was a palatial house with a beautiful garden and a private lake. As I reflected about the Toms, Father said, 'What a terrible fate that family has had. The Soviets deported some of them to Russia during their occupation of Lwów. Those who managed to hide from the Russians back then are sharing the fate of all of us under the Germans. How cruel fate can be! These people gave work and bread to so many families for decades and now the owner himself goes about hungry and hasn't a piece of bread of his own.' We thought about our visitor all that evening. Having heard so much about that family during my childhood, I could not put them out of my mind.

The next day, rumors spread that it might be better to live at one's workplace; in other words, outside the ghetto. Some people even tried to bribe the officials to get a job in such a place in order to be safe. Cill and I went to work as usual. In the afternoon, she picked me up and we went home together.

One day, when she came for me, she handed me the documents of a Christian girl and a necklace bearing a likeness of the Virgin Mary. I took them in amazement and looked them over. One of the papers was a birth certificate in the name of Katarina Haniec of Gola Gora, a small town not far away. There was a certificate from the municipality stating that I was 25 years of age and married. I asked Cill where she

50

had obtained them. Cill told me that Roberto had seen Tama leaving the place without her armband and asked her why she was not afraid to endanger herself this way. In response, she explained that she had bought a Christian girl's documents. Roberto asked her whether she could buy some for me, too. When she said yes, he gave her 1,100 zloty for the purchase – and here they were. That evening, to have a safe place to keep them, I made a special cloth pouch with a cord and hung it around my neck. Then we spent the whole evening thinking of a place where I could go to live. Cill promised to find me one.

The next day, Roberto asked me if I was satisfied now and urged me to find a place to live outside the ghetto. He would keep me fed and entertained; for example, he would take me dancing and to bars. I would be his girlfriend. Even as I nodded, I knew it would be impossible. If I took a room anywhere, I would have to register with the police. In that case, I would have to prove where I came from, and my origins were too close by; I was afraid they would be able to prove the forgery if they investigated. Then Cill reminded me that we knew a woman in the suburbs of Bogdanówka. We decided to go there together.

We walked there the next morning. It was quite a distance. Cill hiked on one side of the road, wearing her armband; I walked on the other side of the road without an armband. I was worried that some passerby might recognize me and turn me in to the Germans. I was afraid that everyone who passed me could hear the pounding of my heart. At last, we reached the place. The woman used to come to our home often, and once she told us that she was hiding a friend at her place. We hoped she would agree to hide me as well. Nobody was around the house; we were not seen entering. The woman listened to us carefully and then told us that she could not take me in for certain reasons, but since we were already there, I could stay the night. I spent the night with her, sharing her only bed in her only room.

Cill returned to work and gave Roberto the address of the

place. He put together a parcel of food and drove to me. When I opened the door for him, the expression on his face and in his eyes told me how glad he was. Stepping farther into the room, he judged my accommodation and looked severely disappointed. After a fine dinner together, we talked for a while and he went back. Later, I realized that the woman disliked the whole affair. She did not want a soldier to enter her room and know that she was hiding someone. She did not even care for the food he had brought. I understood that I had made a mistake. She might have agreed to hide me in her cellar if no one else knew about it. I went back to work the next day and went to the ghetto in the evening. Roberto could not understand why I didn't leave the ghetto, since I had the fake documents. He thought they were enough and I could live wherever I wanted.

That autumn was horrible. Apart from my natural distaste for this season and the routine sufferings, we heard regularly about German *Aktionen* in the ghetto, especially against unemployed people who circulated aimlessly. Old people and children were scarcely seen in the ghetto. They had slowly disappeared. They were always the first to be taken away by the Gestapo and killed.

One Sunday, we were coming home from work with a bottle of cough medicine for Father that one of the Italians had bought for me. As we walked and talked, a Gestapo man ordered us to come over to him and asked for my name and documents. After I handed him my papers, he inspected my handbags, looked me in the eye, and said, 'You're a Christian and you must be going to the ghetto to do business with the Jews. Come with me to the Gestapo.' I was terrified, but Cill held my hand and explained to him that I was her sister and we had medicine for our father with us. We could prove it. He hesitated for a second, not knowing what to do, but at last he let us go.

I usually spent my evenings at home, not even visiting neighbors. Klara, our sister-in-law, visited us often. She lived with three women in a one-room apartment and worked in a shop, sewing and mending clothes. The rest of her family had been killed. Time passed slowly. We had no radio and were always eager to hear news from the battlefield. Newspapers were scarce but always available. We simply could not believe that the Germans had advanced so deeply into Russia and were taking it for granted that they would win the war. What we wanted was for the war to end quickly.

A very cold winter set in. We had no warm clothing and hardly any wood for the stove. We were glad, at least, that Father and Max were working at the flour mill. There they had a place to warm up, bake bread in a very primitive way, and drink warm water.

One morning we woke up to go to work and found the streets covered with ice. The night before, the water on the streets had not drained because the sewers were blocked with dirt. Outside, we could hardly take a step without falling. Cill managed to walk somehow, clinging to Father. In fact, they walked quite well. Cill shouted to me to place my feet firmly on the ice with each stride. The streets were not level and the inclines and declines were very difficult to navigate. Across the street stood a group of young German soldiers who laughed at us with satisfaction whenever one of us slipped and fell. I was enraged. If I only could, I would vent my spleen against these Germans. At last, we made it out of the ghetto and arrived at work.

Sometimes, there were days and weeks when we did not see a Gestapo man in the ghetto. However, I had a premonition: after the period of calm, something would erupt by surprise – a new *Aktion*, perhaps. Sometimes I would see two Gestapo soldiers walking along the street quietly, not looking in our direction, just talking with each other. Sometimes they would stop people returning from work and induct them for some special job, such as unloading their trucks or repairing the fence around the ghetto. After they finished the work, these people were released and sent home. During that quiet period, the ghetto inhabitants breathed a little more easily. Some young couples got married. They were their families' sole survivors and wanted to establish families themselves. In our vicinity, there were only single-family houses surrounded by storerooms and stables. These young couples would decorate the stables by hanging blankets or carpets on the walls and would nail boards over the windows and doors for privacy. We all still hoped that the ordeal would be over soon and we would live normally again.

Spring came, reinvigorating our hope that the Germans would be defeated and we would be saved. We still heard about *Aktionen* in surrounding towns. Father's entire family – his brothers and sisters and their families – lived in nearby Tarnopol.[19] We had heard nothing from them and never mentioned them during the long winter nights. We could not write letters to them and had no idea of their whereabouts.

One afternoon, Father came home from work with our cousin Betty from Tarnopol. She was cute, 22 years old, not very tall, with dark eyes and hair. We were astonished to see her there, and especially to see her in a dirty and shabby dress. She described what she had endured during the previous three days. There had been a major *Aktion* in Tarnopol. She and others were taken away by the Gestapo and placed on a transport to Belzec, a place known to us as an extermination camp. People were incinerated there, as they were in Auschwitz. When the train slowed down on the way, she leaped off, landed in a field of tall wheat, and hid there. Others jumped off as well. The Germans trained their machine guns on them. At first, Betty did not know what had happened to the others, but then she ran into two of them. On their way back to their hometown, they survived on carrots and red beets that they found in the fields until they reached Rawa Ruska, about thirty miles from Lwów, where they slept that night on the floor of an old synagogue.

The next day, Betty headed toward Lwów. She made her way through the fields so as to be able to hide if necessary. At last, she reached town and went directly to our old home on Janowska Street. There, she found new occupants, who told her that we had moved to the ghetto and that my father was working at Tom's flour mill. She found him there, and they came home together.

Cill heated some water, poured it in a bowl, and helped Betty undress. When she took off her blouse, we were shocked to see that she was bruised all over. Some of the bruises were bleeding; others were full of pus and dirt. In several places, her blouse was stuck to the wounds and had to be torn off, causing the bleeding to resume. Cill patiently washed all the wounds and dressed them as effectively as she could. Betty was now the happiest girl in the world because she was with relatives. We had supper together and talked about the whole family.

We tried to convince her to leave the ghetto and live somewhere in town. Her life was at stake, we said. She refused to hear of it. She lacked the courage to do it. Besides, she had no money. She wanted to go back to her mother, sisters, and brothers. She wanted to stay with us for a couple of days only, until she recovered her strength.

The next day, rumors spread that the Gestapo was cooking up something for us. Father's foreman gave him permission to stay overnight at the mill. He received a small room in which he made himself a bed out of some sacks. His meals were the bread that he baked for himself, augmented occasionally by some milk or other food that workers from the outside gave him. Filip took Betty out of the ghetto through a hole in the fence. Then he left her and told her to find a place to hide out. If she were caught in the ghetto, he warned, she would be transported to Belzec. Cill and I also left the ghetto through a hole in the fence. After crawling a long distance in the field, we came at last to Father's mill. To avoid detection, we entered the plant through a back door and spent the whole night hiding in a hallway behind a heap of flour sacks. Whenever workers on the night shift passed by, our hearts stopped. Still, it was better than being in the ghetto.

Early in the morning we knocked on Father's door and went in. He was glad to see us and made hot tea. An hour later, Filip and Max appeared. There had been an *Aktion* in the ghetto, they reported. The Gestapo had rounded up people for a transport, but Filip and Max had escaped and here they were. Later, when we went to work, we told no one about the night we had spent outside the ghetto.

During the day, we sensed something in the air. The Italian soldiers were not behaving as usual. They had a strange sadness in their eyes and faces. Even Sabattini, who was always smiling and joking, was sad. Rutka and I looked at each other. Maria and Henrietta had the same feeling. Everybody was sad. We could not express it in words. Finally, the Italians had to tell us what they knew. It was very hard for them; they liked us and wanted to help if they could, but they could not. The captain in charge of the kitchen stepped out, probably to remind them to tell us. Sabattini and a few others called us over and tried to explain what had happened. We were to leave the place and never return. Orders from headquarters in Rome.

It was a terrible blow for me and the others. We were helpless. I lost my courage for the rest of the day and could not eat a thing. The soldiers tried to do their best to be nice to us. They even cooked a special meal for us, but we couldn't touch it. That evening, we said goodbye. We couldn't find words to explain our plight. The boys felt as if at fault for the situation. We could see that each of them would have spared no effort to help us.

In the meantime, the ghetto fence had been repaired and more guards were assigned to it. The gate was protected by more armed soldiers. Father managed to get jobs for us in the mill, repairing sacks together with two girls who were already working there. We sat on a pile of sacks on the floor and patched the torn ones. One of the girls, Sala, had had her head shaven due to a recent attack of typhus and covered her baldness with a cap. A delicate girl to begin with, she was now very skinny because of her illness. She was the only surviving member of her family; the others had been transported. Our second workmate was Chana, whose husband also worked at the mill and had found her this job. Father made breakfast for us on the stove in his room and we ate it together. He stayed there all week; only on Sunday did he come home with us.

During work, we noticed that the two girls would disappear for various periods of time. After some prodding, they revealed their secret: they were taking flour from the mill to the ghetto and selling it there. It was their way of making money. Every afternoon, a girl named Stasia who worked inside the mill brought a small bag of flour to our workplace, where Sala and Chana had prepared small square bags with strips on the corners. They filled the bags and, before leaving, tied them between their legs and bound them to a girdle in order to carry them easily and undetectably. Stasia, I discovered, was hiding her fiancé, a medical student, and through Sala, who lived in the ghetto, she communicated with his parents. They were always keeping secrets. Later, after we figured the whole thing out, we made the same bags for ourselves and filled them to the brim with flour. It was quite difficult for the first few days to walk home with the bags between our legs, but we got used to it.

Some time later, a new order was handed down: we must not walk to or from work without being escorted by the police or a Christian worker. From then on, one of the workers waited for us in the morning and escorted us to the mill. In the evening, the same man accompanied us to the gate of the ghetto. A few days later, Cill was transferred to another mill near the ghetto. In the evenings, they sometimes sent a truck to take us home. The hardest thing for me was climbing into the truck with the bag of flour between my legs. Father stood near the truck, trembling at the thought of our getting caught with the flour. If we were, he knew, we would all be finished. Several workers stood around the truck, laughing at my efforts to climb aboard. I did it like an old woman: Max jumped into the truck and pulled me by the arm while Father pushed from behind. They also helped the others to climb aboard. At home at night, we emptied the bags into a wooden box. Cill and I sold all the flour we had to a man in the ghetto. The next evening, we carried it to his home in small bags.

I continued bringing home a bag of flour every day. Max even took the risk of packing a side bag with flour and carrying it out. The worst place, one that I always feared, was the ghetto gate, where I was sure the Gestapo sentry would ask Max about his side bag. As we passed the sentry with eyes forward, I thought I could hear the pounding of Max's heart. Only after we had moved far from the gate did we dare to look each other in the eye. Then we felt more at ease. Our wooden box filled up again; soon, we expected, we would pay another visit to the man and sell him its contents.

We went to work the next day as usual – the four of us, Cill, Max, Filip, and myself. As we approached the gate, we saw something going on. The Gestapo soldier was taking aside some of the people who passed through the gate. He simply pointed at someone and said 'Komm komm du,' and these people gathered on the side under heavy guard. Cill, noticing what was happening, moved from one side of the rest of us to the other several times until we reached the gate. She noticed the side from which the soldier took the people and always moved to that side. She wanted to be the victim in order to save the rest of us. She continued to do this on subsequent days, especially when Father was with us.

On one of those days, as we neared the gate, the Gestapo soldier motioned to a man just in front of us. He was an elderly lawyer who now worked at the mill with us. Because he didn't hear well, he used a hearing aid. He didn't look at the guard and didn't hear him calling. I was sure that the Nazi really meant to detain Father. Father had the same idea and intended to turn in that direction. However, the German pointed at the lawyer again. This time, people nearby touched his shoulder and told him that he had been called. The lawyer stepped out of the column and we went on without looking back. We never saw him again.

On the way home that day, we sensed that something was wrong. The streets were empty. As we neared our house, we learned that the Gestapo had conducted an *Aktion* during the day and had swept up all the unemployed and ill. Some of the latter were shot in their sickbeds. Our door was open. They must have searched the house for fugitives. The box where we stored the flour was open and empty. Someone had helped himself to its contents. We would not get the money we had counted on.

There was entertainment at the ghetto gate in those days. Young people with musical talent were recruited from the ranks of the Jewish police and formed an orchestra that performed on command. Now, as we went out in the mornings, we had musical accompaniment. When people were transported from the ghetto, the band played a farewell song. Often the people for whom they played were their own relatives or parents. Most of their repertoire consisted of marches, which resounded in my ears like dirges. I thought of the performers as marionettes whose motions were controlled by someone from above.

Someone told us that a certain factory on Grodecka Street needed workers and that its labor permits were the best and safest of all. We decided to leave the mill and get jobs there. We visited the place one day – a large enterprise housed in a pair of two-story buildings, one in the front of the yard and the other in the back. We found Jews toiling in the latter building, cutting and sewing leather parts. We were hired to join them. For the first few days, we worked in the kitchen, peeling potatoes. The lunch ration in that factory was a bowlful of hot fluid that was called potato soup. It was doled out to the workers one by one, as they queued with bowl in hand.

A week later, we were transferred to a place on Kazimierzowska Street that belonged to the same enterprise. It was a former store with a large show window and two rooms in the back, one of which was the office. There were two desks there. At one sat our manager, a man of about 40. A girl of 18 or so sat at the second desk. Both were Ukrainians. In the second room, there were sacks and bags of pieces of leather. Several girls had already been working there for a few days, cutting pieces of leather by laying steel dies on them and then striking them. We knew the girls and we greeted each other heartily, glad to be together again. The manager came in, gave us dies and a hammer, and explained that we were to produce 700 pieces a day, pack them in a paper bag, and sign the bag. Our output would go to the first factory, which would make it into handbags and sandals.

Olga, the office girl, came to the ghetto gate every morning to escort us to work. We went in groups of four. Apart from Cill and me, there were two sisters, Frida and Chana; an older woman with her daughter; Rachel, Rutka, and two other women. Leaving the ghetto, we saw other escorts standing around, waiting for their workers. Each of them collected his or her workers and left. We were allowed to walk only on the road, even in the smallest groups. The leader walked on the sidewalk. Every day, Max brought us some bread cakes from the mill, where he was still working with Father. I couldn't eat them, so I swapped them with someone else for a slice of bread. Our shift began at 7.00 a.m. and ended at 5.00 p.m. Weak and thin, I was unable to meet the production quota of 700 pieces. In fact, although I had never worked so hard, I seldom completed more than 600. Cill made the rest for me after she finished hers.

The room had a back entrance to the yard. During the day, peasants used this door to bring apples and other fruit into the plant and sell it to the workers. Cill and I had little money and could buy fruit only on rare occasions, such as when we sold our remaining clothing to the peasants.

One day, while we were working, a pretty little ten-year-old girl with blond hair sneaked into the room, sat down near us, and watched us work. We thought she was a child from the neighborhood. She returned the next day and offered to buy us anything we needed. The workers, glad to hear this, gave her money. She returned with tomatoes, fruit, and other things. This went on for a few days, until one day, she was waiting near the entrance when we arrived, and went in with us. Her first question was, 'How is it in the ghetto? Is it quiet?' She could not keep her secret anymore. Her name was Rosa, nicknamed Romka, she said. In the August *Aktion*, she had been taken to the Janowska camp with her mother and brother. When her mother realized that they would not survive there, she gave her a small bag with some valuable gold pieces, hung it around the girl's neck, and told her to go to the German SS officer and tell him that she was a Christian girl who had been taken to the camp by mistake. She had been standing near a Jewish house, watching the scene, and the police had taken her away. She did as told. The officer stared at her, asked her if she was not lying, and sent her out of the camp with a soldier. Her mother had given her the address of a young woman who lived on Goldman Street. She went there and had remained there until now. Her father was in America; he had gone there before the war and could not come back to deliver them from this hell on earth.

After telling us her story, Romka cried and said that it was very difficult for her to stay with the woman because she brought soldiers to her room every night. They drank and sang loudly. She was afraid of them and her heart pounded whenever she saw them. During the day, she was a vagrant, afraid to go to school lest someone recognize her. The manager walked in just then, saw her crying, and ordered her not to come back. If she returned, he warned, he would tell the police. Although Romka didn't come anymore, we sometimes saw her on the street or near our place. She was afraid to come in.

One morning, when we went to work, we sensed again that something was wrong. We heard that the police in the ghetto had been placed on alert. Nobody knew exactly what was going on. We were very tense. No one had anything soothing to say. Everyone wanted to know what was going on in the ghetto and was anxious about the moment when we would have to go back. The hour neared. We went out, formed our groups of four, and headed toward the ghetto. Everyone returned from work at this time of day and everyone had to head down Lokietka Street, the main street in the ghetto, on the way home. The street was lined mostly with two- or three-story buildings with balconies in the front. That day we witnessed one of the greatest tragedies that befell the ghetto. Sixteen of the youngest and nicest boys who served in the Jewish police had been hanged on the balconies of each house in succession. Their hands were bound behind their backs, and a rope wound around their necks was affixed to the balcony. Under each corpse, on the sidewalk, lay a police cap and armband – 16 in a row.

The houses were empty. None of the tenants had returned that day. Gestapo soldiers across the street stared at the dangling corpses and the passersby, eager to see our reaction. An older woman fell on the sidewalk, crying and moaning as she recognized her son. No one walked over to help her get up. She cried that she wanted to kiss her son's legs before they took him away. Cill and I kept on walking. I could not bear to look at those young boys, who had been hanged for no offense at all; they were merely victims of the SS beasts who wanted to show that our lives depended on them and they could toy with us as they pleased. I couldn't sleep that night. The spectacle of those blue-faced hanging bodies remained before my eyes for quite some time.

The next few days were uneventful. We lived one day at a time, going to work as mechanically as robots. There were no *Aktionen* for a while. Several couples got married. The black market continued to operate as usual. People smuggled food and sold it for high prices that some Jews could still afford to pay. Others had no money or anything of value that they could barter for food. They starved.

Early one morning, as we stood in a long column in ranks of four to go to work, we heard that a truck with Gestapo soldiers had parked near the gate. Around the fence, only the Jewish police were in formation, deployed in a chain to make sure that nobody escaped. As if by a prearranged signal, the whole crowd turned and stormed the fence. Within seconds, we had scattered all over the field. There was no sign of the fence that had stood there. The police chased us but we scattered. They caught only a few, the oldest and weakest escapees who could not run fast. Cill and I ran into the first house outside the ghetto and hid under the staircase. We waited there until the last escapees passed the house, the police in pursuit. When the situation calmed down, we went to work without being stopped or checked. Everyone else arrived at work, too. We heard that this particular *Aktion* had targeted young men only. All of them were taken to the Janowska camp.

Our manager was an undistinguished and rather stupid man who knew some Yiddish because, we were told, he had been apprenticed to a Jewish shoemaker in his youth. Although he didn't sympathize with us, he treated us fairly. Olga, a young village girl, was in a big city for the first time. Here she could play the role of assistant manager. She wanted to prove that she was our superior. Occasionally some Ukrainian policeman stepped into her office and let her flirt with him. Whenever this happened, it made her proud.

The police offices were near our factory. Once, Olga came into the room were we worked, crying and shouting that she had lost her wristwatch among the pieces of leather. She insisted on getting it back, never mind how. This meant we had to find it and return it to her. It was an absolute lie, of course, but we were all afraid of what she might do, so we took up a collection and gave her money. She bought herself a wristwatch. Another time, she thought of another trick. To keep her quiet, we collected money again and gave it to her. It turned into a form of blackmail. We paid her and smiled. It was a forced smile, but we had to stay on her good side. Several times, she sat near me and we talked. She told me of her love affairs with Germans and Ukrainian policemen.

Days and weeks passed uneventfully. Everybody knew that a storm would follow the calm. We never knew what the next day would bring. We discussed politics at work and at home. We hoped something would happen so that the world would hear of our suffering and intervene. We hoped the civilized countries would take action against this barbarism. My dream was that the Allied forces would bombard Lwów from the air. Maybe that would bring about a change.

One day, we heard that the police had to assemble at the station in the morning. We didn't know what was going on and who would be their victims this time. Cill and I decided not to return to the ghetto that night. We went to the manager and asked him if we could sleep on the leather bags that night. He could lock us in and leave us behind, we said. He agreed, and after all the others left he locked the front and rear doors.

We lay down on the dirty pieces of leather. We were afraid to turn on a light, had no food, and were terribly hungry. Despite the utter silence, we could not sleep. Our thoughts were in the ghetto. What was happening there? What were they doing to our people? Would we see our dearest ones again? From the nearby police station, we heard noises during the night but could not see a thing. Was it only the police, or did they have other people there? Maybe our manager had locked us inside with the intention of turning us over to the police later! All that night, we spoke to each other in a low whisper. Cill was stronger than I and took me in hand. Be calm, she said. It will turn out all right. The night seemed to last for ages. The first glow of morning light put us more at ease; now we waited impatiently for the other girls to come to work. We heard the key opening the lock and the manager came in. We stepped into our work room and started to work, wishing only to kill time until the others came.

It took them until nine o'clock to arrive, instead of eight as usual. That morning, they told us, as they had lined up to leave the ghetto, they were surrounded by Gestapo soldiers. Others near the gate told them that empty trucks were waiting outside. At a certain moment, the Gestapo men started to hand out square pieces of cloth with the letter 'W' printed on them.[20] 'W', everyone knew, stood for 'Wehrmacht.'[21] The whole crowd pounced on the scraps. Naturally, the strongest pushed the others away and left them empty-handed. Those without the cloths could neither retreat nor run away. Gestapo and SS troops surrounded them and loaded them into trucks. The youngest and strongest were sent to the Janowska camp; the women and the weak were transported to their deaths. The girls who had come to work, of course, were among the holders of the life-giving scraps of cloth. Cill and I were not. Cill decided that we should go to the mill immediately and ask Father what to do.

Olga walked to the main factory to ask whether she could obtain 'W' badges there. She was told that we should wait, since many other workers who had not received them had somehow managed to get to work. Meanwhile, Father obtained the 'W' for us at the mill because we still appeared on their labor rosters, even though we didn't work there anymore. Max, escorted by one of the mill workers, visited us and brought us the 'W.' We tucked the badges away and Cill warned me not to tell anyone about them. If we could get another 'W' from our real employer, she explained, we could give the ones from the mill to others and spare them from having to hide out.

The very next day, we were ordered to report to the main factory. Olga escorted us. Another group of workers there was escorted by a man in his forties, a very intelligent person who had been a lawyer before becoming a foreman in our factory. He sat down and spoke with us. At any moment, we were sure, the director of the main factory would come in and distribute the 'W' badges to his workers. Just then, a woman who lived in our neighborhood came into the room and spoke furtively to her sister. The two of them were older women who were well acquainted with the director. They took their handbags and left – to settle some affairs, they said.

About an hour later – it was afternoon by then – one of the girls stormed into the room and cried that the police were in the yard and around the building. We turned to flee but found that the janitor had locked the door. We begged him to let us out, if only to the attic or the cellar. The room turned into an arena of panic. Some women stormed the windows; others tried to bribe the janitor to let them hide somewhere. It was too late. The police were on the stairs near the door, and near the gate were SS troops with empty streetcars. We showed them our 'W' badges but no one listened. Everyone in this room was to be transported to death. The terrible helplessness that we felt was even worse than in the camp during the August *Aktion*. Back then, we did not know the final destination and still entertained hopes. Now, we knew for sure that we were going on our final trip. We all knew. We had heard a great deal about the death chambers in Belzec and Auschwitz, about how the Germans made soap from our fat and fertilizer from our bones. Cill could not stay still. She pushed her way to the door and cried that we had 'W' badges and were to be let free. Nobody listened. The situation was critical. Every minute was precious, but we could do nothing.

Just then the door opened and the director of the plant entered. He was a young, distinguished-looking man whom I had never seen before. The women surrounded him and cried for help. We could see that he was worried and disgusted. He stared at us and gestured with a finger to a girl who stood near me, then to me, and then to Cill and another two girls. 'Come with me,' he ordered. A few others tried to go with us but were stopped at the door. We went down the steps and followed him into the yard, where another manager – a German civilian – stopped us and wanted to send us back. Our director insisted that everything was all right and led us to the second factory, where a group of men were working at sewing machines. They sat quietly near their machines and looked very sad, probably pondering their own fate.

For a while, the only sound in the room was that of the machines. Then came cries and moans from the other building. Some of the women there leaped from the second-floor balconies. Others shouted to us, asking us to tell their husbands and children what had become of them. We were scared to death. We did not know what we were facing, whether we were safe or whether they would take us and the men away after they were finished with the women in the other building. We stood there sad and pale. At last, all was quiet. No one was outside. The women in the other building were gone. Later we heard that two of them had managed to bribe the janitor, who let them hide in the attic for a while and then turned them over to the SS.

We came home that evening and found Father and Max there. Father cried with joy at the sight of us. Someone at the mill had told him that SS troops had gone to our factory in streetcars and surrounded the place. Father was sure he would never see us again. Our two elderly neighbors who had left the room just before the *Aktion* were also surprised to see us at home. They had been unable to say anything at the time, they explained; otherwise, there would have been panic in the room and they could not have left, and the director would have been punished for letting them escape.

The next day, we returned to our former factory. The girls there were glad to see us back. Rachel told me that when they had seen the streetcars heading in that direction with the SS passengers they had known that something was wrong. They asked their manager, who confirmed it. Rachel removed her armband, oblivious to the mortal danger that this involved, and ran over to the Italians. She told Roberto about the whole situation and asked him to help us, but by now he could do nothing. She came back and cried. Everyone was talking about us. Then the lawyer who had brought the women from the other part of the factory entered. He was in shock, wracked with guilt over having delivered these women to death. Nobody had told him why all these women were being rounded up; he assumed that they would be given 'W' badges and that he would then take them back. Had he known what was awaiting them, he said, he would have fled and let the women disappear. He was an inconsolable wreck of a man after that.

In the ghetto, there were rumors about possibilities of buying a 'W' for 500 zloty, a steep price given our circumstances. People bought the badges anyway, thinking that they might save them. All five of us had 'W's. Others had 'R's, denoting that they worked for the Gestapo or the police. Whatever badge it was, it had to be pinned in a conspicuous place on the front of one's coat or dress.

After a few uneventful days, we heard rumors that every workplace would be assigned a building nearby as a dormitory for its workers. Every workplace now elected a small council, which was to arrange housing for the entire factory population and solve their other problems. Father's mill had a two-story building in the Zamarstynów section of the ghetto. Father was allotted one room there. It was listed as being for the four of us, because we still appeared on the roster of the mill workforce and the rule was that four people were to be assigned to each room.

A small room near Father's was occupied by one Leon, an older man who had spent all his years working at the mill. His job now was to inspect and register all trucks that entered and left the mill with wheat or flour. He had no children, his wife had been killed, and he was alone, so he wanted to live with us. My brother Filip had obtained a room from his employer and shared it with another three workers, but he spent most of his nights with us in our room in an effort to keep the family together. Cill and I slept in one bed; Filip and Max shared another. Father had a cot that he opened for the night and folded up in the morning.

Near us lived a group of girls who worked at the Janowska camp. The badges affixed to their clothing bore yellow numbers. They usually left early in the morning and came back late at night. On our way to work, we saw groups of workers from Janowska marching to their jobs with a police guard on both sides. They looked like skeletons – utterly exhausted, poorly clothed, dirty and unshaven, hardly able to put one foot in front of the other. Such people were always the first to be transported to death, we knew. The Germans would gather the weak and the ill first, take them away, and replace them with new transports. They were shot at Hizla Gora, a range of hills on the outskirts of Lwów that was partly forested and partly covered with sand dunes. The dune area was the killing place. We were told that they sometimes buried people alive. The victims had to dig their own graves and stand near them, whereupon they were shot with machine guns. Those who survived were also thrown into the graves, and others – also from the camp – had to bury them.

The latter never knew when it would be their turn. In fact, after they had done this work several times, they were shot and buried by others.

In one unforgettable incident, as we passed through the ghetto streets one day, we saw two children lying in the street in each other's arms, distended from hunger. Each passerby touched them with a foot to see if they were still alive. They were alive; their convulsions indicated as much. Nobody tried to take care of them; they probably had no family left and were beyond help in any case. The ghetto inhabitants were living skeletons by then, starving and spent.

Gestapo men went from house to house during the day. Anyone found in bed was shot immediately. People in charge of the apartments begged the sick people to go to the hospital, but the latter resisted to the best of their ability. A typhus epidemic was sweeping the ghetto at the time. People with high fevers went into hiding and tried not to let their neighbors notice their condition, lest they be sent to the hospital. They knew that the Gestapo purged the hospital every few days and hauled the patients to the dunes.

Then came a new order: the men were to shave their heads, as the camp inmates did. Now they could no longer escape because they would be identifiable. The men obeyed the order and reported to work the next day with shaved heads. They looked terrible, with their protruding facial bones and sunken eyes. I was terrified that they would order the women and girls to shave their heads as well.

As we sat at home one evening with Leon, the man who lived in the next room, a neighbor came over and shared a rumor: the police had been ordered to get ready for a special assignment the next day. Something was probably in store for us. Father was terrified. It was late and dark outside. We had no place to hide. After a sleepless night, we dressed for work. I pitied poor Father. He had changed so terribly, so unrecognizably. He had always been stout and strong. Now he was thin and weak. That morning he stood quietly, like a child seeking help and protection.

It was early winter. It was still dark early in the morning when we went to the assembly point and fell into line, afraid that the Germans would reveal their secret plan at any moment. We listened to every word, desperate to know what was going on at the gate. We were too far away to see anything, and the mob blocked our vision in any case. We heard from people in front of us that empty trucks with SS troops were standing at the gate. Rutka came over and told me that she had decided to go out with the camp workers because such people surely would not be taken away. I asked her if she had the required sign and number tag. Yes, she replied; she had bought the items in advance because she had heard that these girls, like the male workers, would not be taken away. She walked between our group and the other, still hesitant about which group to join. At last, we were told to go and Rutka stayed with the camp girls.

Our hearts pounded with fear as we neared the gate. The people from the flour mill had already gone out, I heard. This made me feel a little relieved. The orchestra played at the gate, near a mass of SS troops. Outside the gate were numerous trucks on both sides of the road. I tried to look ahead. I was afraid to turn sideways or look behind. The SS men stood in a long row on the side of the street. As we approached them, I was sure we would be taken. Then we passed; they did not stop us. We were outside the gate. Only then did I look to the side. Cill and I stared at each other wordlessly. Our only sensation was relief. Olga escorted us to the factory and we started to work.

Nobody could fill her quota that day. We were depressed, not knowing what was going on in the ghetto. Suddenly, Olga raced into the room, crying. They had killed Rutka, she said. They had decided to transport all the girls from the camp to their deaths that day. As the trucks passed our factory on the way, Rutka had leaped off. A Gestapo guard jumped after her and caught up with her on the sidewalk. He struck her with the butt of his gun and kicked her mercilessly with his boots. Then he lifted her by an arm and leg and threw her onto the truck. We had not witnessed this, but Olga had seen it from the show window in the front room. When she could not bear to watch anymore, she ran into our room. A few minutes later, the manager entered and told us that they were already gone. Poor Rutka had been trying to flee to us, not knowing or thinking what this might have done to us. Had the Gestapo caught her in our place, they would have taken all of us away.

As we marched home through a light snowfall that evening, we noticed that the sky in the direction of the ghetto was red. The ghetto was burning! A large contingent of Gestapo troopers stood at the gate, watching. The nearer we came, the better our view became. The whole section of the ghetto where we had lived until a short time before was ablaze. Much of the street was blocked with corpses covered by a thin blanket of snow. Afraid to look at them as I walked, I stepped on one, moved aside, and stepped on another. They must have been trying to escape the burning houses. Others had been burned alive in the cellars of the buildings. Max had come back to the ghetto alone that day, but Father was still alive, he told us. They had seen the fire from the mill and let Father stay there for the night.

The ghetto was much smaller now. The fence was moved over to contain only the buildings that were still occupied. This was standard procedure. After every *Aktion*, the Germans moved the fence inward, excluding the area that they had 'cleansed'. Thus we were closed in more tightly each time. Now only a third of the original ghetto was left. The rest had been torched.

Several weeks of calm ensued. Sometimes we even went out in the street and met people whom we had not seen for a long time. Once we ran into our former neighbor Benjamin, a shoemaker. He was alone; his entire family had been killed. He now lived in a police building on Pelczinski Street and practiced his trade, repairing boots for the police. He recounted his tragedy and burst into tears as he told us about Berel, his son who had been my age. Berel had been working with his father on the day he was taken away. Benjamin was sure that Berel had only been transported to the Janowska camp and that he would see him again. One day, Benjamin and a few other workers were sent to the attic to straighten it up – and he found some of his son's belongings among the objects there. That was how he found out that his son had been killed. Now he was alone. Sometimes, on Sundays, he received permission to go to the ghetto but had no one to visit there. We invited him to our home, where we spoke about our families and our sufferings.

Camp inmates were allowed to visit the ghetto from time to time, but few of them had anyone left to see and most had no one anywhere. We heard that several factories had furnished the Gestapo with lists of all their workers, who were then taken away and transported directly from work. Rumor had it that the Gestapo had demanded this from the firms in order to eradicate the ghetto population systematically.

Cill was the one who encouraged us to wait for better times. She believed that she would yet be reunited with her husband, Zigi, whom she loved very much. She spoke of him often and refused to be unfaithful to him. She turned down others who propositioned her, even if she might gain by it. One such suitor was a young policeman, a former friend of a friend. As the oldest sister, Cill had a motherly feeling and a sense of responsibility for the house and the family. By now Max had grown up. He was tall but thin. Suffering and hunger had left us all chronically fatigued.

At work, I sometimes stood near the show window in the front room and looked out at the street. I envied the people I saw walking about fearlessly. They were free to go where they pleased and didn't have armbands or numbers on their clothing. I remembered the days when I had been free to circulate. It was such a short time ago, I felt. I would not have been able to imagine even the possibility of losing my freedom. If I were free again, I thought, I would now appreciate that freedom. It was so far-fetched, however, that I could not phrase the thought: the freedom to go wherever I pleased, freedom … I stepped away from the window and went back to work.

That evening, I wrote a letter to Fred, asking him to help me. Perhaps he could find a place for me somewhere. I reminded him of the times we were together and his promises back then to help me out. Rereading the letter, I decided not to send it. I tore it to pieces. I knew he had a weak character and was under the influence of his parents, who were hostile to me. Fearing for his own fate, he would rip the letter to shreds and would not help me. Once, one of his friends in the ghetto had told me that he thought Fred was working for the Gestapo. At the time I thought he had said it just to tease me about my former boyfriend. Now, however, as I wrote the letter, I thought it might be true. In that case, he might promise to help me leave the ghetto and then hand me over to the Gestapo. I though I would choke on my anger.

Work continued as usual, day after unchanging day. I went through the gate twice a day, always with the same fear when I saw the guards.

One evening in February 1943, Leon and the family were sitting together at home discussing politics. People were talking about a huge offensive that the Allied forces were about to mount against the German army. It was the sort of miracle for which we were waiting, the kind that would set us free.

We went to sleep late that night, Cill and I sharing the bed. Suddenly, we heard heavy steps and voices around the house. It was dark outside. Somebody knocked on the door. Father was the first one up. He started sobbing like a child and said, 'They've come to take me now.' He kissed us all. I was not fully awake yet and didn't realize what was going on. From outside I heard a sharp voice: 'Open the door!' Cill opened it and ghetto policemen came in. They had a list. The worst of them – among those whom we knew – was the commander of the group, a man named Golinger. Father was dressed by then, and they told Max to dress as well. Father was still crying, and Max was now, too. Leon ran to the man in charge of the apartments, but he was not in his room. He had gone elsewhere for the night, probably knowing what was about to happen. The rest of us had nothing left to live for. Cill put a coat over her nightshirt and moved to Father's side. Come with us, she said to me. I wanted to obey but wished to dress first. Filip stood near me at a loss. He wanted to go also, but at the last minute he begged me to stay. We might be able to help them from the ghetto, he said. We might get them back. As we stood hesitantly, a policeman entered the room and said to me, 'Hide yourself. You and your sister are on the list, too.' Confused and shocked, I didn't know what to do.

Nobody came for me. The whole two-story house was empty and dark. Everyone had been taken away except for Filip and me. We sat on the bed, not knowing what to do. Then Filip told me to pack up whatever was left. We would go to the apartment where he lived with his co-workers. He had a bed there; we would share it. I took a valise, and we stuffed it as best we could, since we were not allowed to have more than one valise. I packed and cried. I hoped Tom's mill would save Father. Then I heard someone entering the kitchen. I turned around and there, in front of me, stood Max. I cried with joy and kissed him. Filip came over and said, 'Come on, let's get out of here. They may come to look for you. Tell us later how you escaped.'

We stepped out, went a few houses further away, and then entered a two-story building. In one of the rooms on the first floor, Filip pointed to a bed near the window. 'It's ours,' he said. There were seven beds in the room. On the opposite wall were four beds and in the corner stood a small stove. The bed nearest the wall was occupied by a tall man and an 11-year-old boy – his son, it turned out. The next bed was occupied by a man and two lovely children, a girl of five and a boy of three-and-a-half. They were the first children I had seen in a long time, because the Germans killed children first. Children could not work and, worse still, would grow into a future generation of Jews if allowed to live. The boy and girl belonged to a couple who slept in the third bed; the man with whom they shared a bed was their uncle. Next to them slept a young fellow, the sole survivor of his family. In our row, near the window, slept an older woman whose entire family had been killed except for one son, who was at the Janowska camp. On the other side of us were an old woman and her son. Only working people were allowed a place to live and a bed. Relatives had to share.

These people looked at us pityingly as we entered the room. We sat down on the bed and Max told us that the people who had been rounded up were all at the office of the ghetto police. The worst news was that Cill had gone with them. Father might be sent to the Janowska camp – so Max had been told – but for women it was bad. Max then told us about himself. He had gone to the latrine with a few other people and took advantage of the darkness to remain after they had left. A policeman came in and asked if anyone was still there. Max pressed himself to the wall and held his breath. The policeman ran his hand along the walls but missed him. A few minutes later, Max heard no more voices. Everyone had left. He stepped out and came to us. We didn't know what would happen to Father now. Would they shoot him because Max had escaped? And what would become of Cill?

After Max told us his story, we decided to go to work. It was dangerous to be in the ghetto during the day. Filip took Max to his job and I went to mine as usual. In tears, I approached the man who had come to escort us and begged him to save my sister. She worked with us and did not belong to the mill crew, I explained. He promised to do whatever he could. Rachel, one of my co-workers, let me join her column and tried to cheer me up, telling me that everything would turn out fine. I approached the gate in a state of utter dejection. The orchestra played what sounded to me like a dirge. 'Straighten up. Go forward,' I heard Rachel say. 'We're at the gate.' I did as told and passed through the gate. Behind us was a group of men guarded by the Gestapo on both sides. As they neared us, I recognized Father in the first row. His eyes were red as if from crying. I wanted to run toward him, but Rachel stopped me. I studied the look on his face. How pitiful, how tragic it was. I shall never forget it.

When we reached the factory, I sat in a corner and cried. I was cold and shivering. All the girls felt sorry for me; some offered me a bit of bread. I had no food with me but I simply could not swallow a thing. I felt feverish. Rachel put her hand on my forehead and confirmed it. When I left for home at five o'clock that afternoon, I simply could not drag my legs along. Rachel supported me on one side and another girl on the other.

At home, I lay down on the bed in my clothes. I could not move. Filip and Max came back from work. They sat on the edge of the bed and stared at me. I must have typhus, they thought. The woman who used the bed across from ours gave my brother an egg to cook for me. Although I could not remember when I had last had an egg, I couldn't eat. I just tasted the first spoonful and left the rest of it. Max couldn't eat it either. Filip took it for himself and finished it. One of the neighbors cautioned him not to use the same spoon in case I had typhus, but he was too hungry to care. I had the bed to myself that night; Filip and Max sat on chairs next to the bed so as not to catch my fever.

I set out for work the next morning. Filip and Max accompanied me to the assembly point and Rachel took over from there. She was just like my sister Cill, I thought. I felt a little bit better and did as much work as I could. The girls offered me some bread. Filip and Max received a dish of soup at their workplace but had nothing more at home. The family across from our bed had money. They even had roast beef! I aimed envious stares in their direction; if only I could have at least a bone to lick. That day, someone told Filip that Father was in the Janowska camp and would be working at the flour mill again. What is more, the foreman at the mill had promised to remove Father from the camp.

Meanwhile, Cill was in the ghetto prison along with other women. I went there the next day and stood there for quite a while, calling her name. At last, I saw her standing behind a small, barred window. She begged me to get her out. The Germans were going to take them to the sand dunes on Saturday, she had heard. She also told me that a friend of hers who cleaned the street near the prison had brought her a robe. At least she had something to wear now. She asked me again to speak to our foreman or manager. Perhaps they could save her. I promised to do what I could. Back at work, I begged our foreman to do something. He promised to help.

I returned to the prison the next day, a Thursday. Cill told me that the foreman had come and had spoken with her. She hoped he would help her. On Friday, I was there again. This time Cill asked me about Father, Max, and Filip. Then she told me to go away because it was dangerous to be around the prison. Again she begged me to find a way to release her.

I spent Saturday at work, my heart pounding heavily. Olga told us that she had seen trucks under heavy Gestapo guard passing by. The trucks were filled with women, some naked. When we reached the ghetto that evening, I went directly to the prison instead of going home. The prison was empty. I lacked the courage to call Cill's name. My heart pounded like a drum. I circled the prison several times.

Then two policeman came out of the building. One of them approached me and said, 'You must be Cill's sister; you look like her. She went to her death like a heroine. She didn't want to give away her 'W' badge and told us that we wouldn't make any money off of her.' In other words, she had refused to let them strip her of the 'W,' auction it, and pocket the proceeds. 'She was shot on the dunes.'

I didn't answer him. I just looked him in the eye and wondered how he could speak about what had happened as if it were the demise of some drunkard.

I went home in agony and found that Filip and Max already knew about it. We couldn't speak to each other. We just looked into each other's eyes and understood what was in each other's heart. As I sat on the bed, a policeman came into the room with a note from Father. He was in the camp, would be working at the flour mill again, and wanted me to write to him about Cill. I wrote, encouraging him not to let them break him and telling him that Cill had typhus. I didn't have the heart to tell him the truth.

He knew I was lying, though. I received another note from him the next day: 'It's bad for a father to say Kaddish[22] for his own children. I say Kaddish every day for your mother, sisters, and brother.' I held the note in my hands and sobbed. My neighbor in the other bed sat with me to comfort me. She had known my parents well. She told me that her son was in the camp and her husband had been shot on the dunes. He had been one of those who had to dig his own grave. She was alone now. Because her husband used to work for the firm that owned this building, she had received permission to have a bed here. Her only joy in life was when her son occasionally was given permission to visit her in the ghetto.

I met her son the next day. He came to the room, kissed his mother heartily, and took off his camp clothes. His mother set a bowl of water on a chair and washed his back. She kissed him and wept with joy at having him there. He was a nice young boy with an innocent look in his eyes. They sat together and talked. His mother held his hand the whole time.

Filip and Max visited other neighbors in the evenings. I sat in the room on my bed, not wanting to talk to people. Sometimes I had to do the cleaning. I used some kind of gas as a disinfectant. One never knew what illness a person could catch from others. On Sundays, I made soup from flour and vegetables. One day, when I was sitting on the bed, a young man came in and gave me a package. Surprised, I asked him who had sent it. Sabattini, he said. He worked for the Italians and Sabattini had begged him to find me. The man had been circulating in the ghetto for quite some time, asking everyone if they knew a certain Klara who had worked for the Italians. Finally, he found me. I was really surprised that Sabattini remembered me. A year had passed since I had worked there. In the package I found some bread and sweets. The others ate well that day. I ate nothing; I simply could not find any taste in that food. Instead, I saved part of my portion for Father.

The Gestapo entered the ghetto frequently to check if any of the people who were supposed to be in the camp were hiding out there and to inspect the inhabitants' work cards. Whenever such a visit was impending, the news spread very quickly by word of mouth. Our neighbors who had children rushed them to another room and hid them behind a large wardrobe. Sometimes the Gestapo entered apartments even without being ordered to do so by their officers. In these cases, whenever they caught somebody not working, or found workers' wives or mothers, they were bribed and allowed the people to go free. Most of these soldiers were Poles who lived near the German border or Ukrainians serving in the Gestapo. They were *Volksdeutsche*,[23] of German origin, and they held German citizenship. Real Germans were not easily bribed, for they considered it honorable to be barbaric toward Jews.

One night, Max went up to the attic to sleep because we were told that the house would be searched and he had no labor permit. Indeed, two Gestapo soldiers entered early in the morning. Suddenly I heard Max crying and calling me. Running out, I saw one of the Gestapo men holding Max tightly. Filip ran out to see the man in charge of the company for which they worked. Meanwhile, in tears, I begged the Gestapo men to let him go. They did so. By the time Filip returned, Max was back in our room, seated on the bed. He told us that he had heard voices and steps and was sure that it was time to get up for work. Since he no longer owned a watch, he came down from the attic and ran into the arms of the Gestapo. It was too late to retreat or escape. Now that it was over, I made some tea and sweetened it with some saccharin that we had bought on the black market in the ghetto. We drank it and went to work.

Father continued working at the flour mill for a short time. He and the others in his group were taken there from the Janowska camp. Olga sometimes came with me to see him at the mill. On each such occasion, he asked me to escape from the ghetto into the fields, to anywhere my eyes might lead me. That might give me a chance to survive. He told me that he passed our house on Stokowa Street every day and saw the fruit trees in bloom. I wanted very much to see it for myself. It had been two years since we had been forced out of our home. Olga agreed to come with me.

We went down Janowska Street, Olga on the sidewalk and I on the road. On the way, Olga told me about her adventures and her successes with the soldiers. We approached the house. Yes, the flowers and trees were in full bloom. My heart felt as if it were being pressed in a vise. My memory flashed back to the time when my brothers had planted those trees and told us that we would eat their fruit three years on. All we had had time to enjoy were a few apples from one tree. Olga kept talking but I blocked her out. I was too busy with my memories. One of our old neighbors, an old woman, crossed herself as if in prayer upon seeing me still alive. Another woman said that she had seen my father pass by on his way to work and that the sight of him in his current condition made her heart ache. We went back to work and later I went home with the other girls.

The next day, I heard that the ghetto police would be bringing the people from the camp to the public bathhouse on Sunday. The bathhouse was not far from the ghetto and our home, I knew. Near our home, the fence was damaged. A few boards were missing and others were loose. Anyone could slip through easily. That day, I waited with some others for the camp people to come back from the bathhouse. They all entered the ghetto together with the police. They were told where to meet later to go back to the camp. I took Father straight to our room. Seating himself on the bed, he expressed his disgust with the situation and told us to run away. Perhaps we would survive.

As we sat and talked, somebody gave a signal that Gestapo men were in the building. My father was terribly scared; he was there without permission, after all. I raced with him to the balcony, pushed him into the lavatory, and stayed near the door. Two Gestapo soldiers came into the room and then stepped onto the balcony. They looked at me and went away. They must have thought I was waiting my turn to enter the lavatory. There were only two lavatories on the floor and so many people used them. That night, Father returned to the camp with the others.

I liked the two children who slept across from us and would spend time with them, telling them fairy tales. These innocent children were accustomed to running away and hiding like mice upon every alarm. They didn't even understand why. I felt so sorry for them.

The woman to my left, who shared her bed with her son, felt ill one day and could hardly get up. Although she finally forced herself to get up and dress, I could see that she was feverish. She still had a high temperature the next day but she got up anyway, afraid to remain in bed. I was sure she had typhus. I begged her to go the hospital, but she ignored me. There were seven beds in this room and 14 people slept in them. The people in charge of the building took charge of the matter and insisted that she go to the hospital. How terrible it must have been for her son, sharing a bed with his mother and knowing she had typhus. He visited the hospital to find out exactly when the Germans had last transported the patients away and to determine what the hospital staff knew about *Aktionen*. He came back and assured his mother that the hospital had just been cleared out and would be free of *Aktionen* for the next week. She would recover in three or four days and would come back, he said. She wanted assurance that her hair would not be shaved off. They had promised him this, too, her son said. Only then did she agree to go to the hospital.

Her son took her over the next day. He visited her later and found that she felt better and wanted to come home. The hospital staff told him to leave her there for another day or two; she would be well by then, they said. Two days later, he went to visit her. When he returned, he told me that she was no longer there. Early that morning, all the patients had been transported to their deaths. He sat on the bed, depressed and speechless. We had no words to console him.

It was quiet now in the ghetto, but we heard that the Germans were liquidating ghettos in other big cities. The

Warsaw ghetto uprising[24] was over and people said that our turn would come. Filip and Max told me that if I could find a place to escape to, they would also be better able to try something. At work, I asked Rachel for her advice. She told me that she was planning to escape to a village and work for the peasants but that I could not go with her; I was too delicate for that kind of life. I didn't know what those people expected of a girl when they hid her, she explained. 'I can't advise you because I myself don't know what to do,' she said.

People in the ghetto met in the streets and asked each other for advice. Everywhere people were being caught by the Germans or denounced by others. We were exhausted and looked terrible. Just by looking at us you could see that we were from the ghetto. We were like living corpses, seeking help and not knowing where to turn.

Now the Janowska camp was sealed. Nobody was allowed to leave. Father no longer worked in the mill. Filip returned from work one day and told me that the Germans were liquidating the camp. Someone had told him that a fleet of trucks had taken the inmates to the dunes to be shot to death. I didn't sleep that night. I was waiting for a miracle. Perhaps Father had survived and would send us a note. Indeed, we received a note – not from Father but from Leon. Father's last words, he reported, had been uttered to an SS man: 'I can still work. I'm still strong enough to work.' 'We don't need you anymore,' the SS man had replied.

For days and nights I was haunted by Father's face and the last words that he had blurted out to the German, his eyes red from crying: I can still work.

Our neighbors, the ones with the children, now bought some Cian-Kali, a poison that was very expensive in the ghetto. I saw the mother put it in their children's pockets and tell them to swallow it if the Germans took them away. I looked at them enviously. They had Cian-Kali, other neighbors had bought some for themselves, and we couldn't afford it. I pitied the small children and the mother who had to prepare them to take their own lives.

6 Escape

One day in late May 1943, Filip handed me his remaining money and told me that he had spoken with two people about me. The first was a woman who had worked for us as a housemaid. Her name was Kasia and she lived in a three-room, Jewish-owned apartment on Magazynów Street. She agreed to take me in. If this proved impossible, a friend of Filip's who lived on Behma Street had promised to hide me in his cellar. On 1 June, I packed a small bag with some clothes and family pictures and decided to try my luck. I said goodbye to Filip and Max. They said they would also try to escape, since I would not be with them.

I went to work as usual. In the afternoon, when the other girls collected their things to go home, I took my belongings and climbed to the attic without telling anybody. Finding the door locked, I sat down on the last step and waited impatiently for everyone to leave, my heart pounding. Once I heard somebody coming up the stairs; it must be for me, I thought incorrectly. About an hour later, I removed my 'W' and my armband and went out. I had to pass near the police station. Policemen stood outside the gate. Most of them knew me because they used to come into the factory. I tried to find another way behind the building, but there were several policemen standing there, too. I couldn't retreat now, though; I had to continue. I passed right in front of the police, eyes straight ahead.

I reached Kasia's house about twenty minutes later. Kasia opened the door when I knocked. She had been waiting for me impatiently. In her apartment, I met a former neighbor of ours, Mrs Spacirer, the mother of my girlfriend Lotty. I was very glad to see her. We kissed. Her husband had been arrested by the Soviets during their occupation of Lwów between 1939 and 1941. He owned a barbershop that had served quite a few policemen, and his friendly relations with the police made the Soviets suspect him of being against them. One of Mrs Spacirer's daughters was killed by the Germans together with her husband. A son was killed by a German car accidentally. Now she had only one son left, and he was there in the apartment with us.

The next day, I asked Kasia to go near the ghetto to see my brothers and give them some of the money that I still had. She refused to go just then but promised to go the next day. She went to the ghetto the next morning but was unable to make contact with anyone. The previous night, soldiers had surrounded the ghetto and removed all its inhabitants. When Kasia returned with this news, I took it as a fatal blow. I had hoped that my brothers would escape to the woods or the fields. Still I waited, imagining that they might knock on the door at night. They knew where I was, after all. But nobody came.

The next day, we had to hide behind a wardrobe twice when we saw Ukrainian policemen entering the building. Two days later, a brother of Kasia's visited her from the countryside. He spent two nights with her and then left. After he left, Kasia asked us to go away because of what she had seen on posters on the walls: the whole family of anyone caught hiding a Jew would be shot. At first, she merely asked us to leave, but later she threatened to turn us over to the police. I begged her to let us stay until the next day.

I decided to go to the second address that my brother had given me, that of his friend on Behma Street. Mrs Spacirer cried bitterly; she had no money and nowhere to go. She begged me to let her join me if I found a hideout. Mundek, her son, told me that were it not for his mother, he would try to save himself by hiding in the sewers or somewhere else. I went to bed that night wondering where I would be spending the next night. Would I succeed in finding another place at all?

That night I dreamed that my father had given me a big, fat chicken to eat. I shared the dream with Mrs Spacirer. It was a very good sign, she said. A gift from the dead is good luck. Although I was not superstitious, her words strengthened and encouraged me. I wanted to believe her, to believe anything that gave me hope. Late that afternoon, I kissed Kasia and Mrs Spacirer goodbye, gathered up my things, and left.

I was not far from our old home, and I had to pass through streets where almost everyone knew me. The market where we had bought our vegetables was on Behma Street. I was afraid someone would recognize me and call the police. I made it to the right house but nobody answered my knock on the door. A woman came out another door, told me that the residents were not home, and slammed her door. I had to go somewhere else. It was late; curfew was nine o'clock.

I walked to Krola Leszczynskiego Street, where Andzia, a woman who cleaned the office where I had worked during the Soviet occupation, lived. She was very grateful to me back then, because I had helped her get the job. Usually she did house-cleaning and laundry for some families in our neighborhood. She liked me very much; she used to tell everybody in the office how she had carried me in her arms and nursed me when I was a child. When she came to work, she would clean my shoes and brush my coat, wanting me to look pretty and cleanly dressed. I knew she had only one room, which served her as both bedroom and kitchen. All I wanted, however, was to sleep there that night. Although Krola Leszczynskiego Street was only a few blocks away, to get there I had to walk along streets that I used to take every day on my way to the public school on Kordeckiego Street, which I had attended for seven years; to my friend Ada's house on Grodecka Street; and to the big stores where my parents used to do their shopping. I knew all those streets well. Nothing had changed there. At last, I found Andzia's apartment. I entered the gate and turned toward her room.

The door was half-open. Everything looked neat and clean.

A vase with flowers was on the table. No one was there, however. I sat down to wait, and a few minutes later Andzia walked in. She looked younger and nicer than I remembered. Seeing me sitting there, she was shocked for a moment. Then she asked me whether anyone had seen me enter. I answered in the negative and said, 'Andzia, dear, let me sleep here just this night. It's late and curfew time is coming. I have nowhere to spend the night.'

'I can't, my dear child,' she replied. 'You see, I married an old railway worker and he comes home late at night. Sometimes he's drunk, and if he finds you here, he may kill you and me, too. He beats me when he's drunk and I'm afraid of him. But try to go to your Aunt Risha's apartment. A neighbor is living there and I know her husband won't come home tonight because he went to Rawa Ruska.'[25]

To get there, I knew, I had to go through a narrow street and then to Pierackiego Street. Andzia advised me to leave my bag with her until I found another place. I took only my handbag and a larger leather handbag. I stuffed the smaller bag into the larger one. I put a kerchief on my head and left everything else with her. Andzia accompanied me to the house but said that she couldn't go in because she and the woman there were not on speaking terms.

I went upstairs. I knew the apartment well. I had been there often visiting my aunt and uncle. In a flash of memory, I recalled how I used to knock on the door and my aunt would open it for me. Her little daughters had liked me very much; they jumped on me and kissed me whenever I visited. The smaller one, Chanale, was proud when she was told that she looked like me.

The door opened. I recognized the woman with no difficulty. She also identified me at once. Her first words were Kasia's: had anyone had seen me coming there? I offered to pay her as much as she wanted for that night and for that night only. She demanded 100 zloty; I agreed. Then I told her how I had come there. What troubled her the most was that I had left the bag with my things with Andzia. If I were captured, Andzia would have them. Several times, she asked me what I had brought. My big, gray leather handbag lay on a chair. She stared at it the whole time. Obviously she liked it very much. She liked my kerchief, too. I gave them to her and kept only the small red handbag, in which I had some pictures and documents.

The building was occupied by railway workers who came home late. Three times that night, I heard steps outside and each time I plunged under the bed in fear. I didn't sleep that night. Neither did my host. She was worried. If somebody had seen me enter, we could both be turned in to the Germans. Early the next morning we dressed and had tea. Then I paid her the 100 zloty. This impressed her, perhaps because she had thought I would break my promise. She told me that if I failed to find another place to sleep that night, I could return.

Before I left, she gave me a small handkerchief. I pressed it to my mouth as if I were suffering from a toothache. That way, I would not have to look up and no one would recognize me. I said goodbye. She said, 'My poor child. I wish you the best of luck.'

It was still very early in the morning. People were rushing to work and nobody paid any attention to me. I decided to walk to the palace where the Italians had their headquarters and try to find a cellar to hide in. I couldn't even begin to think about what would be later. I moved along main streets, trying to avoid policemen by crossing over whenever I spotted one. There was no turning back. I reached the palace but could not enter; the place was fenced securely. I went a few buildings farther, to the apartment of the captain in charge of the mess. I would beg him to help me somehow.

I went up to the second floor, pleased not to have been spotted. I stood at his door for quite some time, hesitant and too scared to knock. He might come out by himself, I thought. Eventually I mustered all my courage and knocked. An older officer, a corpulent man, opened the door, and I asked for Captain Campanini. The man said he was not there; he had gone to Warsaw. I didn't know enough Italian to ask any further questions. Instead, I returned to the palace in the hope of spotting Sabattini, or some other member of the old staff, in the yard.

As I stood at the fence, a German soldier approached me and said, 'Zeig dein ausweis' (Show me your identification). I stared at him as if I didn't understand. 'Niks verstchen,' I said, affecting a Polish accent and mangling the German grammar. He repeated his demand, adding that a woman from a house nearby had sent him to me. 'She said you are a Jew.' I laughed at him for a second and showed him my Polish identification and the necklace with the Virgin Mary that I wore around my neck. He was a soldier in a tank unit, not a Gestapo man. He probably couldn't even read the birth certificate that I handed him. He looked around for a policeman.

Every second I stayed with him was dangerous, I knew. If a policeman or Gestapo agent appeared, I was done for. I wasn't registered with the police on the basis of this birth certificate, and in the meantime the police had issued new cards called *Kenkarte*.[26] Nearby, an Italian soldier whom I didn't know walked by. In a split second, I pocketed my birth certificate, turned toward the Italian, and clutched him by the arm. He looked at me in puzzlement. I told him that I was a Jew and that he must help me. I asked him to call Sabattini, who worked in the mess. I don't know how much of my Italian he understood, but he figured out the part about calling Sabattini. The German soldier stood there and watched as I walked away with the Italian. Finally, he left.

The Italian led me to the mess but Sabattini wasn't there. Two young soldiers told me to wait; he might come later. I understood little of what they said. The soldiers didn't know me but, as I found out later, they had heard about me from others who used to talk about me in the mess. One of the soldiers went to the colonel, the same officer who had disliked me because I had told Rutka not to go to his apartment to work for him. Without coming out, the colonel sent me an order: Leave at once.

Where should I go now? I remembered Olga. Perhaps she would let me spend a few nights with her. She lived in Sknilów,[27] an area out of town. To get there, I would ordinarily take Grodecka and Bogdanówka Streets, but this time I wanted to avoid the main streets. I found a street that circumvented Grodecka, a quiet street without pedestrians or even passing cars. Every house carried a sign with a skull and crossbones emblem and the message 'Eintritt verboten' (entry forbidden) underneath. I had made a mistake: I had stumbled into the neighborhood where the SS had either its quarters or offices. I didn't know the way out of the area. On the street corners were more signs with skulls and crossbones and the same message. I heard only the echo of my own footsteps. At any moment, I feared, an SS man might step out of a building and arrest me or even kill me on the spot. I had no choice but to keep going. At last, I reached the main road to Sknilów. Although my legs were trembling, I felt more at ease.

I hadn't gone far when I looked back and saw a Ukrainian policeman on a bicycle approaching me from behind. I stopped and asked him if he knew where a family named Matwejow lived. My idea was to avert his suspicion by getting in the first word. It didn't work. He asked me to show him identification. It was no use showing him my false birth certificate. Instead, I told him the truth: I had a card but there was no point in showing it to him because I was a Jew. I had exhausted my power to fight for my freedom. He could take whatever money I still had and shoot me. But I begged him, 'Please, do it here, on the spot. Please don't take me to the Gestapo. They'll beat and torture me first. Put yourself in my shoes,' I said. 'Or imagine that your sister were in my place and that your people were undergoing this instead of mine. You were born a Ukrainian and I was born a Jew. We didn't choose our nationalities.'

I saw him hesitating. He had a difficult decision to make. He said to me, 'Tell me where other Jews are hiding and I'll let you go.'

I didn't know, I said. I had escaped by myself.

'Where did you sleep last night?'

'On Hizla Gora,' I answered. 'I hid in the bushes.'

A man approached us and told him that he had seen a Jew hiding in the wheat in that field. The policeman told me to stand still. If I moved, he would shoot me. He pointed his rifle in the direction of the field and went to the place that the man had indicated. The person there turned out to be not a Jew but an old shepherd with a goat. He sat there watching it as it grazed.

The policeman returned to me. He asked to repeat the name of the family that I was looking for. It was just a name that had come to mind, I said. 'I just asked you because I thought it would take your mind off me.'

He told me that actually he hadn't been coming after me at all. He had found a young boy standing on the street crying; his mother, seeing a policeman, had left him there and run away. He had mounted his bicycle to look for the mother and encountered me on the way. He told me to follow him off the main road to a narrow street. I asked him if he had come from the police station on Kazimierzowska Street. Yes, he said. I told him that I used to work in the factory near the station and asked him to give my regards to one of the policemen there. I was calm, even knowing that if he took me away now, he would shoot me. It was all the same to me.

We turned onto a narrow path in the field. He was still hesitant and didn't know what to do with me. At last, he told me to stay where I was. He raised his rifle, fired a shot, jumped on his bike, and rode away. For a moment, I was in shock. I did not know if I was alive, dead, or injured. I saw no blood and felt no pain. I ran after him; I wanted him to shoot me again. But he rode off without even glancing back. I rested for a while until I had recovered from the shock and then continued toward Olga's house.

A policeman on a motorcycle passed me but paid me no attention. I was scared. Few people were on that road. Almost everyone was at work. At last, I saw a woman standing near a house and asked her for the address of the Matwejow family.

They lived in the house opposite hers, she said. She pointed it out to me.

I stepped into a spacious yard and knocked on the door. Olga's mother opened it. I asked for Olga. She said that Olga was not at home and invited me to come in. I told her my story and begged her to let me spend the night. Her other daughter joined her at the door, listened to my tragic story, and asked if anyone had seen me enter their house. No one had, I assured them. Olga's mother went to the kitchen and brought me a dish of potato soup. If she would let me hide there, I said, I would give them our property after the war was over. By that, I meant the house we had lived in on Stokowa Street. She listened for a moment and said that her husband would never agree to that. She would let me sleep in the attic that night – there was some straw up there – and would not even mention my presence to Olga or her husband. I would have to leave early in the morning. I agreed and climbed to the attic, afraid that her husband would find me and throw me out or that the woman from the other house would call the police. While thinking of the danger, I fell asleep.

I slipped out quietly before sunrise the next morning. Where should I go? What should I do? I sat in the field under a tree, thinking about my past. I had no future. I had lost most of the pictures that I had saved during my escapes, but I still had a few. Two of them were of Fred. On the back of the first one, he had written, 'To Klara, with love,' and had signed his name: Alfred Gwozdziewicz. Once I was proud and ambitious. Now, I thought, I could only go to his house and beg him to help me. Perhaps he would let me spend one night in his home. Later, I would see what I could do.

I was afraid to stay where I was; somebody might notice me and call the police. I continued on my way, stopping at a few houses and asking if I could rent a room. All the people I asked looked at me suspiciously and said they had none. They looked at me as if I were condemned to death. Perhaps that was how I looked. My coat was torn and dirty, its fur collar ripped. The straw on which I had slept must have left its marks. At one house, I asked for some water. The people there gave me a glass of milk. I offered to pay for it but they turned me down. They also gave me directions to town and showed me how to avoid the police. I thanked them and headed in the direction that they had indicated. It seemed to be a very long way. I had to cross fields and hills known as Listopadowe Gory. I could hardly climb the hills in my weakened state. I was emaciated; my skirt was tied with a string to prevent it from falling down. I wore a green woolen blouse under the coat. The soles of my shoes were torn, and my feet hurt whenever I stepped on a stone. I thought about Fred. How should I enter his house? What should I tell him? It was a holiday; I knew Fred would be home. I rehearsed what I would tell him. Suddenly I felt a stab of fear. He lived at 72 Grodecka Street. Grodecka was the main street on the way to the railway station; it was always crowded with German soldiers and police. I tried to picture Fred's house as I had seen it two years earlier: the stairs leading to the first floor and the brown door on the right. His mother was a tall, fat woman. She might not let me in; maybe she would slam the door in my face. I would have to take the risk.

Although I was engrossed in my thoughts, struggling to climb the hills, and exhausted after three sleepless nights, I noticed two men and a woman approaching me from a distance. They watched me struggle to climb the hill and called out words of encouragement: 'Another step, another step and you'll make it.' I stared at them and thought I recognized Fred as one of them. I banished the thought, thinking it a figment of my imagination. I had been thinking too much about him in the past few hours. I climbed the last few yards on all fours and neared the threesome. Seeing me approach, they turned their heads away. One of them was really Fred. I smiled at him bitterly and continued on my way.

It seemed funny. I was not angry at him for his behavior. I was comforted by the thought that I no longer had to turn to him, humiliate myself, beg him to help me, and be refused. Now I began to fear him. He might send a policeman to arrest me. I knew that he and his friends had recognized me. They knew we had once been in love for a long time. Knowing his weak character, I suspected that he was afraid I might approach and talk to him. That would get him into trouble. His conscience must be troubling him, I thought, for the way he had just treated me. Back in the old times, I had helped him solve his problems. Frightened, I quickly put distance between myself and them, not looking back.

I was back in town now, on Leona Sapiechy Street. My last chance might be the Italians. I wondered how I would make it to their headquarters, which were far away on the other end of town. There were not many people in the streets. Military cars passed by. I made a decision: if I could not reach the place, I would throw myself under the wheels of the rushing cars and end it all. I couldn't bear any more suffering.

From Leona Sapiechy Street I had to follow Pelczynska Street. One of the worst prisons in town was located there; nobody who entered it came out alive. The cells were under-ground and flooded with water. Thousands of prisoners died there. An armed Gestapo guard stood near the prison entrance. My heart pounded violently. I thought it might be best to go behind him and avoid meeting him face to face, but few people passed that way and I didn't want to attract atten-tion. Then he turned his back to me. In a flash I decided to slip behind him, and I succeeded.

It was still a long way to the Italians, though. The next obstacle was a German police station. There were few people on those streets. Luckily, I passed the station uneventfully and came to Zielona Street, where the Italians' palace was located. It was a very long street. Once I saw a Ukrainian policeman. I bent down to tie my shoe. After he passed, I got up and spotted another one coming. This time, I stepped into the first building I reached and knocked on the door. A woman opened it for me. I told her that someone had recommended her to me and said she had shoes to sell. She glared at me suspiciously and said it must be a mistake; she had no shoes to sell. I apologized and returned to the street. The policeman had gone away. I was very tired and wanted to rest somewhere, but there was no place to sit down. I passed a kiosk and bought three rolls. When the salesman handed them to me, he gave me a suspicious look. I paid him quickly, stepped into the first building I saw, and ate the rolls hastily. They filled me with new vigor.

I reached the palace. A guard stood at the gate, so I crossed the street to the palace garden. I saw a lawn, a large number of trees, and a fence made of wire mesh. A tall soldier in an Italian uniform was shooting at birds with a rifle. I approached the fence and studied him. Perhaps he was one of the soldiers I had known from when I worked there. He noticed me and came over. I asked him if Sabattini still worked in the mess. No, he replied. He spoke a little German and asked if I was that girl, Klara, of whom he had heard so much. I told him I was.

'You know,' he said, 'the colonel sent us yesterday to search for you and gave us a package of food for you. He was very sorry that he had to send you away, but you came through the main gate and if the guards and other soldiers had seen you enter, they could say that he was hiding Jews. He had to send you away. I'm the chef of the mess. I'll tell you what I'll do for you. Come back tonight at nine o'clock. I'll lift the fence at this spot and we'll take you in. Then we'll figure out what to do with you.' He told me to wait for him a second and then brought me a package of sweets. I took it and went away.

Again, I faced the problem of where to go. I was terribly scared. Here I was, so close to salvation but with many hours to wait. I had to sit down somewhere. I was so tired that my eyes were going dark. I went over to some children playing in a nearby park and gave them the sweets. The children sat down around me and asked me where I lived and what I was doing there. I told them that I had come from a village called Gola Gora, and that my train back would be leaving late that night. I had to wait here in the meantime. The children wanted to come with me to the train. I took out my pictures and showed them to the children. I was glad that I was seated amidst these youngsters, who believed my story and whom I didn't have to fear. After a while, one of their mothers came over and called her child away. Later, other mothers did the same. I was alone now. Since I was suspicious of the parents and now realized that it was a private park, I knew I had to leave right away.

How could I wait until nine o'clock? I trembled from head to toe in fear of being caught by the barbaric Germans. I went into a field and came across a girl grazing her goat. I told her the same story, that I was waiting for my train. I just wanted to pass the time. I was also afraid to stay there too long; the people who lived around the field knew each other and would be suspicious of a stranger. I left and walked toward the palace again. It was early but I had no choice, no where else to go.

An Italian sergeant came toward me. I wanted to know what time it was, so I asked him in Italian: 'Che ore sono?' Eight-thirty, he answered. That put me at ease: another half hour to wait. He didn't go away. He asked if I knew Italian and then offered to accompany me. 'No,' I answered. 'I'm traveling.' 'That's all right,' he said. 'I'll go with you to the train.' I couldn't shake him off, and it would soon be time to go to the fence. I told him in Italian, as best I could, that it was dangerous to be in my company because I was a Jew, an *Ebrea.*[28] He looked at me in amazement. Finally, he commented, 'Oh, now I understand why you looked so scared and turned away when that German soldier passed by here.' It was the same sergeant whom I had seen the day before. Apparently he hadn't understood me then. He took out his wallet and began to withdraw some banknotes. I told him I couldn't accept the money because it was worthless to me. 'I'm with you right now,' I said, 'but after a while, when I leave you, I may be arrested and sent to my death. Your money won't save me. Better keep it.' This made a tremendous impression on him. He asked me if he could do anything to help me, said something else that I didn't understand, and then walked away quickly.

I moved toward the rendezvous point near the fence. The soldier who had promised to let me in was already there with a comrade. Deeper in the garden, I saw another two soldiers. The man had organized a contingent of six soldiers, his best and most trusted friends, so that I could enter without being seen by the wrong people. They led me to the attic, where I sat down, satisfied at last that I had a place to sleep. Giovanni, the tallest of the soldiers, was from near the Yugoslavian border. A lovely man, he brought me bread, salami, and other food. I wanted to eat everything, but when I started I felt unable to swallow. I had to get used to eating again after such a long period of starvation.

I asked the soldiers for some water to wash myself. Hearing them washing dishes in the kitchen downstairs, I remembered when I used to work there. I looked around and spotted the place in the attic where my sister and I had slept one night, after the August *Aktion* the year before. Nothing had changed there, but so much else had happened, I had suffered such tragedies in my life. The soldiers finished their work downstairs; it was quiet there now.

Giovanni came upstairs and told me that he would now ask his officer what to do with me. That frightened me; the officer might order me to leave then and there. I begged Giovanni to let me sleep there just that night. I'd leave the next day, I promised. Noticing my fear, he assured me that all six soldiers were close friends and that their officer was their friend as well. He was a very intelligent man and would surely help me. He told me again that I had nothing to worry about; they would take care of me in every way. Impatient now, I waited to see what they would do with me.

Around midnight, Giovanni returned with two of his friends. They helped me down from the attic and gave me an army coat and cap to wear. I understood from their conversation that an army car was waiting near the hole in the fence and would deliver me to a small room in their camp. They drove me to the camp, left me in the car, and went to see if the path to the room was clear. After a while, they returned and took me with them. We entered a building, went upstairs quietly to the first floor, and headed down a long, dark corridor to what looked like a storage room. It was filled with packed crates. In a corner was a pile of green military coats with white fur linings. They told me to sleep on the pile and then went away. I was still scared; my experiences had made this feeling chronic. I shuddered at the sound of voices or footsteps in the corridor. However, I fell asleep quickly because I was so tired.

I woke up early the next morning and pondered my fate. What now? About an hour later, the door was unlocked and Giovanni entered with an officer. The officer told him to open another door, which led to another very small room. Then he ordered Giovanni to screw in a blue light bulb and leave it burning day and night. They dragged a bed into the room, hung a small mirror on the wall, and brought a bowl of water for washing and a bucket for personal use. I entered the room and sat down on the bed. The Italians left, but after a while a soldier came in with food. I learned that his name was Fosco; he was the cook and one of the six soldiers who had taken me in.

I had an unexpected visitor that afternoon, the sergeant whom I had asked the time the day before. He told me that he had left me and run to the camp to call his friends in order to work out how to hide me and save me. When he returned to the place where he had left me, I had gone. He was a bunkmate of the soldiers who had brought me in. When they came in late at night, he told them about me. They listened to him carefully and told him not to worry about me any more; I was hidden safely, not far away. They also told him that they had watched him talking to me back then but could not divulge their plans until they could determine how to carry them out.

He told me about himself. His name was Mario. He was married and had a family. A bricklayer by trade, he lived in a village near Bologna. Mario was so excited to see me there that he wanted to do something to make me feel happy and contented. He took off his silver ring, which he had made as a souvenir from a Polish coin. He gave it to me, together with a figurine of a hunchback that he kept on a necklace as a lucky charm. Hang it on your necklace, he said. It will bring you luck, too.

From then on, the two men came to visit me frequently. Fosco brought my meals; Sergeant Mario changed the water in the bowl and talked with me to keep me company. Sometimes Giovanni came by to see if I was comfortable and asked me if I needed anything. They brought me two new army shirts, which meant that I could now wash my own shirt in the bowl. Once they handed me a package. Inside, I found a pair of wooden sandals. My own shoes were torn and they wanted to surprise me. I was very weak then and slept a great deal in the day and at night. The soldiers who knew where I was would sit in a room nearby playing the guitar or singing. I knew they were doing it for me, to make me happy.

I lay in bed thinking of my family and their fate – how their lives had ended. I recalled seeing my boyfriend, Fred, again and remembered how he had turned away from me without a word. That hurt. Why had he turned away? Why did he, along with the Germans, condemn me to death? Didn't he know I was innocent? Was my Old Testament religion enough reason to condemn me? Everybody knew that Hitler's cause was not limited to his country's internal struggles. He wanted to rule the world. He had chosen us as the first victims because we were a minority. He had sent his forces to fight the Poles, too. He had sent Poles to camps in Germany, and many of them were also killed. Fred, as a Pole, was also under German occupation. I thought about that a great deal. I wanted so much to write him a letter, to prove to him that there were still good people in the world, that good people feel much better than those who turn their heads away. Good people, I wanted to tell him, can look anyone straight in the eyes without feeling guilty.

I stood up and went to the small window. Across the way was a convent, and there were nuns dressed in white in the yard. Some of them were sitting together on the green lawn. Everything around them was quiet. By now I couldn't sleep as much as I had at first. I lay on my bed, tortured by thoughts of my past years and sufferings, reliving it all in my mind. The room was too small to move around in. I just lay on the bed, trying to sleep, and counted the days. I had been there for five days, I knew, but I had no firm grasp of days or time. I couldn't talk much with the soldiers because I wasn't fluent in Italian. I could communicate only with those who spoke a little German.

I heard the key turn in the lock of the front room. I wasn't as afraid as I had been. Now I trusted these people; I was sure that they wanted to help me. Hearing footsteps in the front room, I waited for the men to come in. I liked these people. They understood me, knew my people's fate, and wanted to save me from the barbaric Nazis. The door opened and I saw Sabattini with Giovanni. Giovanni must have brought him here without telling him about me. Sabattini stood in the doorway, shocked and confused. Then he came to my bed, kneeled, kissed my hands, and wept with joy. I did the same. He had always been so good to me and to all the Jews who worked in his mess. I felt about him as I would about an older brother. He would be leaving for Italy the next day, he told me. The others would join him later, and he would wait for me there and help me in all ways. He sat with me for a while and then left. Giovanni went with him and locked me in.

Seeing Sabattini made me feel so good and comforted. Now, I also knew that they planned to take me with them to Italy. I hadn't given a thought to the next step; it was enough to have food and a place to sleep.

Fosco brought me supper that evening, and Giovanni and Mario came to visit. They sat on the bed and talked. 'We're going home,' they said. Giovanni would stay for another couple of days with his officer. They also told me that the Germans would be coming in two days to inspect the place and see the rooms. I had nothing to fear, they promised. Their officer would lead the Germans around and show them what he wanted them to see.

My room would be closed and locked. I was somewhat anxious but trusted them to take good care of me.

The two days passed. I heard the sound of jackboots in the building. I held my breath and waited to see what would happen. After a while, they entered the front room. I heard voices in German. To me, the language alone made it seem as if the men were saying, 'Murder them'; 'Kill them'; 'Murder them'; 'Kill them.' Every German face looked the same to me, with that uniform and steel helmet. I had come to regard Germans as heartless, tough, and devoid of conscience. I wondered how they behaved in their private lives, with their families, wives, and children. The sound of someone rattling the door handle stopped my reverie. Someone said, 'Klave' (key). The Italian soldiers ran downstairs to look for the key to my room. The Germans stood at my door for a few minutes. I was ready to jump into the convent yard at the sound of the key opening my door, but instead they left a few minutes later.

That evening, the soldiers told me that their officer had sent them to look for the key but told the Germans that there was no point in it, since it was the same small room as the one they had seen downstairs. The soldiers were pleased to have duped the Germans, for whom they had little affection. They often brawled with Germans in cafés and remembered how Germany had treated their country in the First World War. The soldiers didn't like Mussolini either, since most of them were anti-Fascist workers and peasants.

They would be leaving in just three days. Would they really take me with them? How would they conceal me in transit? How would they get me across the border? The next afternoon, Fosco and Mario came to my room with a small valise. They explained that when I detrained in Italy, I would have to mingle with the other people at the station and go outside with them. Carrying the valise, I would look like a passenger. They also gave me some Italian currency for my immediate needs. If I were detained by the police there, they cautioned, I must tell the truth and admit that I was Jewish; otherwise, I might be taken for a spy. Fosco told me his home address and made me repeat it several times in order to commit it to memory. He also warned me not to reveal the names of any soldiers of my acquaintance if I were caught. The Italians don't kill Jews, he added. I had nothing to be afraid of. At the worst, they might put me in a special concentration camp with other Jews. There, people who had to travel received permission and were allowed to leave the camp.

They came to my room the day before they had to leave. Giovanni was with them. They were trying to figure out how to put me aboard a train without my being seen or recognized. I didn't understand everything they said but I could see the concern in their faces. At last, they told me to roll up the blankets and mattress and wait for them; they would talk it over with their officer. I didn't have a watch, but they seemed to be taking a long time and it was very late. They would be leaving for Italy early the next morning. I was impatient to know my verdict. Had they forgotten about me? As I paced nervously by my bed, I heard the door to the front room being opened. Then my door opened and Giovanni entered. He told me to put on an army coat and a beret. It was midnight, he said. 'We're taking you to the train now. The others will board tomorrow morning and the train will set out for Italy. We had a long talk with our officer. We were looking for the best way to take you to the train safely.'

I gathered the blankets and put on the coat and cap. For the first time, I put on the wooden sandals that they had bought me. It was hard for me to walk in them; I had to walk softly and they were noisy. When we went downstairs, Fosco saw two soldiers in the street, heading in our direction. He motioned me to stop near the gate. The soldiers passed by, arm in arm and singing loudly. They were probably drunk and happy to be returning to their families. We avoided the narrow pedestrian gate and went to the wide gate used for cars. A half-track stood there, its rear opening toward us. I stepped into the truck, without even seeing who the driver was. Fosco boarded with me and the truck pulled out. On the way, I saw only a few German soldiers on the streets. It was late; all of Lwów was asleep.

We reached the railroad terminal known as 'Die Wiener Station.'[29] Trains shuttled back and forth. The station was brightly lit and full of German soldiers. I was scared again, seeing so many Germans around. The truck approached a long row of cars and turned around with its rear to the door of one of them. I stepped straight into the car, which I found filled with crates. Inside was a soldier with a rifle, on guard. I was led to the center of the wagon. Fosco and Giovanni said something to the guard that I didn't understand. I presumed that they were telling him I would have to stay there.

The soldier, a short, swarthy fellow, asked me how much I had paid for my trip to Italy and to whom I had paid it. I had paid no one a thing, I answered. The people who had arranged my passage did so out of sheer humanity, to save me from death. I didn't like his question about the payment. I was afraid to share the car with him but even more afraid when he left me alone for some time. He might disclose my presence there to someone. When he returned, I tried to explain to him – as best I could in Italian – that the officer in charge of the transport knew about me, thinking that this would give him more respect for me. I didn't sleep that night; I wished the night would be over and the train would move.

I spoke with the soldier as the hours went by slowly. He told me he was from Corsica. He couldn't possibly go home now, because the British and the Americans were there. When he got back to Italy, he would get his furlough and remain there. He asked me if I were going to somebody in particular. I had no one there, I said, but I wanted to leave Poland and would figure out the rest later.

The time passed. I heard trucks approaching. They must be carrying the soldiers. I felt relieved now; the soldiers were my benefactors and I felt secure with them around. I heard them calling to each other. They climbed into my car and loaded other cars. Fosco and a comrade came over to me and said that the train would be leaving in the afternoon. Giovanni and the officer would join them a week later.

7 To Italy

The train did leave in the afternoon. As we passed through open fields and forests, the Corsican tried to get friendly with me. I could join him for his furlough in Italy, he offered. He even tried to embrace me. I pushed him away. Late that afternoon, the train stopped in a field and the soldiers got out to stretch. Fosco and the others visited me and asked me how I felt. I told them that I was afraid of the Corsican soldier. They looked at each other and promised to take care of it. After a while, I saw them outside talking with the Corsican. Then the four of them came into my car with their gear and the Corsican removed his and went to another car. I never saw him again.

As the train rolled along, Fosco and his friends described Italy and told me what a lovely country it was. Fosco also told me about his family. He had two sisters and an older brother, and the four of lived harmoniously. Tina, the younger sister, was a dressmaker, and Lidia, the older one, helped her in her work. His brother, Vittorio, held an office job. Fosco showed me pictures of his girlfriend, Lucia, and asked me what I thought of her. Naturally, I said she was very pretty. Back on the topic of Italy, Fosco offered to take me to the movies and the theater and promised me that I would enjoy life.

I nodded after every word but was engrossed in my own thoughts. I saw the fields and observed how nice and green they were. So many fields, I thought, and so much space. How many people could settle in these fields and make a good living! Instead, they're killing each other. What for? The world is so big, but not big enough to find room for these innocent people. Must they be killed? The greenery and the wonderful scenery filled me with such sadness. My brothers and sisters would never see those sights again. They had been so young. I sighed heavily and wondered, tears filling my eyes, whether there would be more wars after this one.

The soldiers were talking with each other – about me, I presumed. They were concerned about what I could do and where could I work. I paid little attention to them. I had always liked nature and was charmed by green fields and woods. The train was moving quickly now. We crossed Czechoslovakia and moved into Austria. The soldiers informed me that we would eventually reach Italy via the Tyrol area and end the trip in Pontebba. We were into our second day. I slept on a large pile of blankets behind a wall of crates. When the train was in motion, I could sit near the open door and enjoy the view. When it stopped, I went behind the crates to avoid discovery.

At one of the stops, I heard Roberto's voice. He was walking in the field with a little dog. I also heard someone calling him. I asked the soldiers to bring Roberto to me. I had once worked with him, I said. They didn't approve. He was a Sicilian, they explained, and was therefore untrustworthy. I understood their intentions and thanked them for their kindness and good advice.

The train moved again. Our next stop was Vienna. When we approached the station, I hid behind the crates. The train made a longer stop here than elsewhere. Then we entered the Tyrol area, not far from Italy. The scenery was as stunning as I had seen it in the movies – pine-forested hills with houses below. I couldn't stop admiring the view. As we passed an intersection, I saw a man in Tyrolean dress riding a bicycle. Why did these people have the right to live while my parents, brothers, and sisters did not? I couldn't ask anybody that question; no one could answer it. However, my aching heart and the suffering I had endured wouldn't let me forget it. My family was always on my mind.

We pulled into Pontebba late at night. The railway station was brightly illuminated and festooned with flags; a band played the Italian national anthem to welcome the returning soldiers. When the train stopped, the soldiers jumped off and closed the door to my car. From then on, I heard only their singing and shouting. I had the impression that they were being served drinks and sandwiches. My heart was beating quickly now. I sat in the unlit car alone, entertaining all kinds of thoughts. For one thing, I was worried when I heard approaching footsteps. Was it an inspection? Somebody tried to open the door of the car but could not. He went away. I wished the soldiers would come back, but they didn't.

Suddenly, the train moved and changed rails. A grim thought struck me: the train must be returning to Poland, perhaps to pick up the rest of the soldiers. What would become of me now? They might find me and hand me over to the Germans. I decided not to return to Poland, come what may. I would leap from the train. But instead, the train stopped. Happy now, I heard the soldiers' voices and footsteps. They opened the car and told me that we would be continuing on to Udine. It would take another three hours. They stayed with me for the rest of the trip. They said that a boy was hidden in the cabin of a truck that had been placed aboard the train. Later, two Russian boys were also found on the train.

We moved on. I was relieved not to have to return to Poland or jump off the train in the dark. Fosco told me his address again and gave me other instructions: how to leave the train, how to reach his family, and how to act if caught by the police.

We arrived at Udine at 10.00 a.m. The train stopped in a field outside the station. Now the soldiers were worried. How could I get out, there in the open, without being caught? The other soldiers left the train in groups. Fosco stepped out of the car with the others in his party. A few minutes later, they appeared on the opposite side of the car, where no one could be seen. They opened the door, carried me down in their arms, told me to go forward, and ran back to their group. I stood still for a second and then walked in the direction I had been told.

105

After I had gone only a short distance, I was stopped by a soldier on guard. He asked me what I was doing there and explained that this was a military depot. I couldn't answer him. I stammered a few words that he didn't understand well. Finally, he told me to follow him. It turned out to be quite a distance. I could hardly walk in my wooden sandals; furthermore, it was a hot day and I was wet with perspiration. He accompanied me to a police station and turned me over to a policeman.

The staff at the station were Blackshirts, members of a special militia. I was afraid that I had fallen into Fascist hands. I was ordered to sit down and wait for their officer. One of the men asked me if I wanted to wash and pointed to a spigot. I opened my valise, took out a piece of soap that the soldiers had given me, and washed my hands and face. The policeman, noticing that I had a few pieces of soap, asked me if I would give him one. Soap was hard to obtain in Italy at the time. Later he asked if I was hungry and took me to a nearby restaurant. I ate only fruit.

On the way back to the station with him, I felt much more confident. I wasn't afraid of the Blackshirts anymore, given the way they were treating me. The officer arrived and started questioning me. He told a policeman to check my valise. Inside, he found only my coat, a towel, and a few pieces of soap. In my handbag they found some Polish documents and my family pictures. They inspected the photos and asked me to identify each person in them. The interrogation proceeded in a very friendly manner. Finally, the officer asked me to explain how I had got there. He had already marked down the time of arrival and place of origin of the train. Since we didn't understand each other very well, a young priest who spoke a little German was summoned to interpret.

In my story, I identified myself by the name that appeared in my false Polish documents. I wouldn't have been able to prove that I had another name, even if I had wanted to. I said that I had boarded the train at the main terminal in Lwów without having being seen by anybody. The officer wrote everything down verbatim. Then he asked me why I had taken the trip. I told him that my entire family had been killed and that the Germans had sent us to Germany for forced labor. I did not tell him the whole truth because I thought that he, as a Fascist, would send me back to the Germans. And I omitted all mention of the Italian soldiers.

The priest interpreted everything I said but changed a few sentences to slant the case in my favor. They were all very kind to me. I was bewildered. Generally speaking, I knew police only from their worst side. Anyone who served in the police force, I imagined, had to be harsh, unkind, and untrusting, especially if he was a Fascist. During their occupation of my country, the Soviets had told us only bad things about the Fascists. After the interrogation, the priest left and the officer gave the policeman some orders that I didn't understand.

The policeman asked me to go with him to a streetcar. I didn't know where he was taking me now, but I was sure that it was not to prison. In the streetcar, I stood on the front platform. Passengers stared at me but I wasn't afraid as I had been in Poland. At a certain point, we stepped off the streetcar and walked to a hospital. The policeman told me that I would be in the company of 30 Russian girls.

In the hospital, a nun took charge of me. The policeman told her about me and left. The nun told me that there was another woman from Poland there and I would have company. I had to exchange all my clothing for hospital clothes; my own had to be disinfected. I would have to spend several weeks there, the nun said, to make sure I did not have any disease. She ushered me to a bathroom and invited me take a hot bath, which refreshed me after my three-day journey by rail.

Later, the nun led me to a room with two beds and introduced me to a young woman who called herself Maria. I identified myself as Kasia, as shown on my Polish I.D. card and documents. Maria asked me when I had arrived. Just this morning, I replied. She said she had been there for two days. She made a special effort to prove that she was Christian like me. We looked into each other's eyes without saying another word.

After a while, we opened up to each other. She sat on my bed and we talked about ourselves. Maria told me that she was married; her husband, a doctor, was off in Russia in the army. She came from a small town in Poland. Her father had been an engineer who worked for one of the Judenräte during the German occupation. The Germans had ordered him to draw a plan for a gallows. The facility was built to his specifications and he was the first one to be hanged on it. The Germans had killed her mother, too. She had a sister and a brother in Lwów, hiding in the home of the Italian officer who had helped her come to Udine. She had managed to detrain without being detected and walked into town. She found herself at a loss, on the streets of a strange city among strangers. Looking around, she saw a lovely garden nearby. Its gate bore the name-plate of an army colonel. She pressed the bell. The owner opened the door himself. After she entered and told him her story, he invited her to stay in his home until he determined what he could do for her. The next day, he asked the police investigation officer for advice and was told to send her to the hospital. According to the story that she had told the investigation officer, an Italian officer with whom she had fallen in love in Poland had helped her to escape to Italy. She was desperate to save them. The colonel had promised to help her, and indeed, he wrote a letter to an officer of his acquaintance who was stationed in Lwów, asking him to bring them over to Italy.

As we conversed, the nun knocked on the door and invited us to the dining room for supper. The food was excellent; the table was nicely set with napkins, forks, knives, and china. I could hardly remember when I had last been served in that manner. Afterwards, with little to do there, we circulated among the rooms and visited the patients. The nun noticed us and warned us to stop doing that; there are contagious diseases in the hospital, she said. We paid no attention to her. Having gone through so much already, I was sure that nothing could hurt me anymore. My room-mate and I had so much to tell each other that we sat up until late at night.

Two days later, the nun brought in another young woman who introduced herself as Jamina. Because she was an Italian officer's wife, she received special treatment. Her meals were served to her in her room and her husband visited her every day. 'I came here with my husband. We have to go to Rome, but first I've got to spend 15 days in the hospital, under observation. Tell me about yourself.'

'Oh, I fell in love with an Italian soldier, but I can't find him now,' I replied. 'He came here two weeks ago and I managed to come here too, but I don't remember his address. I only know that it's in Parma. After I'm discharged, I'll go there and find him.' Jamina advised me about how I might do that. One day, she introduced me to her husband and told him my story. He promised to help me find my fiancé. I tried to wriggle out of the situation by telling him that I wasn't sure he still loved me. Perhaps he had a girlfriend and had forgotten about me. I couldn't give him anyone's name, but I assured him that I would find him myself after my discharge.

Jamina's parents lived in Poland; she read me letters that she had received from them and told me about the dog that she had had there. She loved the animal very much. Her parents were *Volksdeutsche* and great German patriots. She hated Maria from the moment she saw her. 'She's a Jewess,' she hissed. 'Avoid her.' Now that Jamina proved to be a venomous anti-Semite, I was in a very delicate situation. I tried to tell her that Maria was a Christian, that she said her prayers every night while kneeling near her bed. 'I'm sure you're mistaken about her,' I said. Jamina refused to budge and attempted to prove her suspicions by telling me various things that she 'knew' about Jews.

Maria gave me no peace either, asking me why I was hanging around with Jamina and accusing me of having told Jamina that she was Jewish. If Jamina denounced her, she would tell her that I was Jewish, too, she said. At a loss for what to do, I stayed in my room to avoid them both. Jamina, however, refused to take no for an answer. She would call me to her room and ask me to take walks with her in the garden. I was afraid of her now. She took my story seriously and was making efforts to track down my non-existent fiancé and to denounce Maria.

Jamina was an unusual woman. She liked to walk with me to the other side of the garden, where soldiers who were probably convalescents sat on benches. She took a particular liking to one who looked African, a type seldom seen in Poland, where people tend to be fair-skinned and blond. It made me wonder. Her husband was a nice, young, intelligent guy. They had just married. Jamina showed us some of her family pictures, including one of her husband in a black uniform sat on a horse. Maria approached us just then, and Jamina showed the picture to her. She looked at it and blurted, 'Oh, your husband is a Fascist.'

'Yes,' answered Jamina. 'You don't like it?'

I felt that Maria had said the word unwittingly; it had just slipped out. She wiggled out of the situation by changing the subject. On Sunday, Maria went with me to the hospital church.

The tension between Jamina and Maria grew worse from day to day. Maria always blamed me for this and threatened to tell Jamina that I was Jewish and had lied about myself. Despite her fetching appearance, I realized that Maria was self-centered.

One day, I was summoned by the investigation officer. This came as a surprise to me. When I went in, the clerk told me that I had been called there to give a statement about whether Maria was Jewish or not. Jamina's husband was there; he had denounced her. If she proved to be Jewish, she would have to go to one of the special camps that the Italians had established for Jews. I told him that the accusation was false and that it reflected Jamina's personal dislike of Maria. I had gone to church with Maria and saw her pray every night before she went to bed. The clerk said that he shared Jamina's suspicion because he had been in Vienna before the war and had met Jewish girls who looked like her. I denied the whole thing, returned to my room, and said nothing about it to Maria. She would never believe it. Instead, I told her that I had been summoned to give some information about myself.

I learned that day that Jamina would be leaving the hospital the next day. I took that as good news, but Maria still warned me. Her jealousy and egotism gave her no peace. As Jamina packed the next day, she asked me again for my fiancé's name. Again I thanked her and said I would find him myself. Before she left, she gave me 100 lire that her husband had left for me, wrote down her address, and asked me to write to her. She didn't even say goodbye to Maria, although she promised to give me a message for her just before leaving. Maria was very eager to know what she had to tell her. She approached me every few minutes and asked me again and again. I couldn't get rid of her. At long last, Jamina's husband came with a car to pick up his wife. Then Jamina shared her secret: she had denounced Maria and I should tell her that. Maria stood nearby, eager to hear what Jamina had said. I told her that she would find out after Jamina left. We said goodbye again and they drove off.

I felt as though a stone had been lifted from my heart. The ten days that I had spent with her had been hell on earth. Maria still wanted to know what she had said. She threatened me again and was nasty to me, but I held my silence. After a few days, Maria calmed down and spoke with me as if nothing had happened.

One day, a young woman named Stefa was brought to the hospital. She happened to be from the same town as Maria and was a refugee like us. She told us that she had been arrested in Pontebba and had been forced to share a room with prostitutes, thieves, and underworld types. She had fallen ill and had been sent to the hospital. As a detainee, she feared that she might be sent back to Poland. Happy with the way things had turned out, she befriended Maria and the two of them shared memories of their home town.

The colonel who was acquainted with Maria came to visit her several times with his wife. On one such visit, they gave her material for a dress, and the next day they took her to a dressmaker. When she returned, she told me that the dressmaker was closely acquainted with a Polish woman who was married to an Italian and had been living in Udine for a long time. I wanted very much to meet her. We had nobody to visit. Besides, we had been told that we would be transferred to a convent and would be under constant observation by the police investigation officer unless an Italian citizen took responsibility for us. Although the colonel had agreed to do this for Maria, she was reluctant to give me the Polish woman's address. She wanted to reserve the spot in the convent for her sister in Poland, just in case she managed to come over. Maria regretted having told me about her.

The 15 days passed and we were transferred to a convent in the same town. We were given a room together and were allowed to circulate outside. In the convent, we met the 30 Russian girls of whom I had been told on the way to the hospital. It turned out that they were working for the Italians against the Russians, as spies or in other capacities. One of them was pregnant and her fiancé, an Italian soldier, came to visit her often. Several of them were married to men serving in the army of the Russian general Vlasov, who had surrendered to the Germans and subsequently fought against the Russians in alliance with the German army. We became acquainted with all of them. I was amazed to see these young girls, who had grown up under the Communist regime and had probably been members of the Komsomol pioneering youth organization, and now were traitors against their own country. Why?

The next day, Maria and I went into town for a walk. This was the first time I had been in the street unescorted and without having to be afraid of Germans. I walked around like anyone else, free. I peered into shop windows and stared at the people. 'Stop smiling,' Maria warned. 'People are looking at you.'

'I'm really smiling?' I said, wondering. I didn't feel that way. I was simply experiencing the thrill of feeling free.

We were told that the police investigation office would buy us clothes. A nun went out every day with another group of Russian girls to buy the most essential items. Finally, our turn came and a nun went with us. We went from shop to shop. Maria had some money of her own and wanted to buy more than the necessities. We received underwear and shoes. I chose a pair of red summer shoes; Maria took the same. Later, she asked the nun to help her buy some material for a dress. The nun was very patient and went wherever we asked. The townspeople looked at us in puzzlement: two adults being led by a nun?

On our way back, we passed some military billets. After we had gone some distance from them, a soldier on a bicycle came up behind us and handed Maria a newspaper, saying that his officer had sent it to us and that we had forgotten it in the shop. He turned around and went back. Maria opened the paper. In the margin, someone had written, 'Why are you in the company of a nun? When can we meet you?' The nun saw it, too, but held her silence. Later, she said to us, 'I can see that the two of you are Christians. You're behaving well, not like the other girls, who don't know how to behave and are as loud as Jews.' We said nothing. I only felt a kind of pressure in my throat.

How ignorant people were. They lived only with such knowledge as they had acquired from others, giving no thought to the truth. Poorly read, they had no idea how many famous people all over the world subscribed to the Jewish faith. They didn't know that Jews had given the world medical discoveries and inventions; nor did they know how much Jews had contributed to the music and theater that they enjoyed in their everyday lives. We are no different from others, except that we belong to that minority whose ancestors did not accept the New Testament. These were my thoughts as we walked back to the convent wordlessly after the nun said what she said.

Maria and I were no longer on good terms. She was the acquisitive type who wanted others to serve her whether they wished to or not. I was not the sort of person she wanted me to be. I was a hard nut for her to crack. It was hot, humid, and stuffy in our first-floor room; the windows opened toward the houses across the way and mosquitoes bothered us at night. One night I was so badly bitten on the face that the next day I looked as though I had the measles. Another night, it was so hot that I soaked my sheets in water to cool off. When Maria couldn't sleep, she would wake me up and make me keep her company. One night, she heard a steady dripping sound and decided that someone had embedded a recording device in the wall. After we got out of bed and turned on the light, we found that it was a leaking pipe.

We took our food to our room and ate it there. In the dining room, the orphan children – girls who lived and attended school there – ate first. The Russian girls occupied the dining room next because they were a large group; they also slept together in a large hall. The orphans were not allowed to fraternize with the Russian girls because of the latter's behavior on the street and in the convent.

One day, Maria asked me to join her for a walk in town. On the way, I asked her if we could visit the Polish woman whom her dressmaker had mentioned. It would be good to get acquainted with someone in town, I said. Maria's initial reluctance yielded after some persuasion. We found the woman's address. It appeared to be a fruit shop. We entered and introduced ourselves. 'I'm Marysia,' said the woman, 'and this is my husband, Ludwig. We're pleased to meet you.' They seemed to be about 45 years of age. We spoke in Polish, which Marysia's husband understood, although he didn't speak the language. He had been born in Italy, and his real name was Luigi. However, he had spent some time in Lwów, where he had met his wife and married her. Then they had moved to Italy, where they had been living for a long time. The store was nice and neat. I noticed a room in the back with its own door.

We were pleased to meet these people and spent several hours with them. Marysia asked us to come back and see her often. She enjoyed talking to us, she said. It was late when we left; we rushed back to the convent because they had announced a show that evening that we wanted to see. By the time we arrived the show was over. The star had been a magician whom the police had sent especially for us girls. Maria was mad at me. It was my fault, she said; we shouldn't have visited that couple today. I knew her well enough by then to take no umbrage when she turned her tongue on me. Still, I found it tough to be with her. She was unfriendly and very false. I wanted to make friends with two Russian sisters, 16 and 18 years old. They were nice, cute girls. Their father had been a doctor until their whole family was murdered. Since then, the two sisters were inseparable, never mixing with the other girls in their group. One of them played the piano, always choosing sad music. I sat together with them.

A few days later, I visited Marysia by myself. She was delighted to see me and her husband was so pleased that he kissed my hand in greeting. Marysia asked me to tell her about myself. Naturally, I introduced myself as Katarina Haniec of Gola Gora, 25 years of age and married. My husband had been drafted into the Soviet army. I told her that I was a Ukrainian (as stated on my false birth certificate). Hearing that, Marysia said she was also Ukrainian and proposed that we continue the conversation in that language. I explained that my parents were a mixed couple and that my Polish mother had given me a Polish education. Marysia asked me all kinds of questions about Lwów and people she still remembered there. I had supper with her and her husband and then went back to the convent.

Eventually, Maria found a job in a laboratory and went to work every morning. I would visit Marysia. One evening, when we returned to the convent, the nun told us that a fellow who introduced himself as a Pole had phoned us twice. He was very lonely and wanted us to visit him. He gave a military billet as his address. Maria didn't want to go but urged me to see him. The next day, I told Marysia about the man; she also encouraged me to visit him and prepared a package of fruit for the occasion.

I went to the address that afternoon. At the gate of the camp, I asked the guard for the name that I had been given: Zygmund Walczyk. The guard told me that he was a refugee from Poland and then told someone to call him for me. Zygmund came out. His face lit up as though we were old friends. He asked me to wait a few minutes, went inside to ask an officer for permission to leave the camp, and returned with a smile. He was wearing a military uniform without insignia. When I asked him why he wore a uniform, he explained that he had nothing else to wear.

He spoke enthusiastically about his Polish homeland. He missed the Polish fields terribly, he said. I looked him straight in the eye and said that I was glad another soul had been saved from that hell. Zygmund stared at me in amazement, unable to believe his ears. He had assumed that I was a Christian and had been afraid to speak with me frankly. Hearing my words, he trusted me and said, 'Kasia, can you help me find out what became of a girl from Lwów? She's 19 years old and her name is Klara.'

I was astonished. How could he know about me? 'How were you told about Klara?' I asked.

Zygmund explained that he had escaped from Lwów by hiding in the cab of a truck that had been loaded aboard a train. After being hospitalized for 15 days, he was assigned to a room with a group of soldiers. Before leaving for home, the soldiers had asked him to find out what had become of that girl and to write to them with the information. They were worried, Zygmund said, because they had seen her being arrested. They had searched and asked for her everywhere, but nobody had seen or heard of her.

I smiled and solved the riddle. 'I am Klara,' I said, 'but now my name is Katarina Haniec.' Zygmund said he would write to the soldiers that very evening. As we walked, Zygmund described his own tragedy and ordeal. He had an aunt in London, whom he planned to join her after the war. After a lengthy walk, I gave him Marysia's address and said that he could always find me there.

I went back to the convent. That night we had an air raid. It was Udine's first experience with aerial bombardment and the townspeople were unaccustomed to it. When they heard the sirens, instead of going to the cellars, they ran into the fields. Even the soldiers left their billets to join them. Some people even brought parcels containing their most important clothes with them. I headed in the same direction as everyone else. When I reached the fields, I had the impression that the whole town was there, although some people had climbed aboard trucks and left town altogether. When the all-clear siren sounded, everyone returned.

At the fruit store the next day, Marysia told me that she had thrown her bedcovers and wardrobe out the window, thinking the whole town was being bombed. She also explained how to use the scale and told me the prices of every item. She introduced me to her customers and said I was 25 years old. It was unbelievable, they said: I looked 18 and was a *bella carina*. 'That's how Polish girls look,' Marysia said proudly. When there were no customers in the store, we sorted the fruit and removed the spoiled ones. Later, we packed sweets in bags to be ready for the customers. Whenever customers came in, I served them. While we were packing the sweets, I told Marysia about Zygmund and said that he was lonely in the billets. He didn't know a soul and had no money. She urged me to invite him to the store.

She and her husband would spend the whole day at the store, going home only at night. She did her cooking on a small stove in an adjacent room that also served as a storeroom for crates of fruit. In the evening, after closing the store, she cut grass for some rabbits that she was raising at home. Her husband would go out early in the morning to buy the fruit and would come back at noon. Luigi/Ludwig always greeted me with a kiss on the hand. I knew he was doing it to be nice, but I didn't like it much. One day, Marysia decided to go with me to buy material for a dress, but Luigi insisted on taking me instead. On the way, he urged me to leave the convent and move in with them. I told him that I couldn't do this without permission from the police investigation department. He would have to present a written undertaking to be responsible for me. Luigi took me to a store where I chose material for a dress and skirt. People in the store stared at us curiously; they probably knew him and wondered what he was doing in the company of a woman my age. We returned to his shop and Marysia decided to go with me to the dressmaker.

On the way, she took me to their apartment. I had never been there before. We crossed a large yard and then went up some stairs. She unlocked the door and we went in. There was only one room. The beds were unmade. The furniture was new but the room looked shabby and untidy. There was a big mirror on the wall. I looked at my reflection. I hadn't seen myself in a mirror for a long time; I had only seen my reflection in a windowpane when I combed my hair. Marysia changed her clothes and locked the door as we left. We went downstairs into a narrow hallway, where she opened a door and let me into a small room. This must be the kitchen, I thought, although it looked like a storeroom. As it turned out, this was where Marysia kept her rabbits in cages. They were white with gleaming red eyes. Grass was strewn around them. A few boxes nearby were also filled with grass. She put some more grass in the cages and we went out.

On our way, Marysia told me that she would like to visit her relatives in Poland after the war. If I stayed with them until then, she continued, I could come with her. 'I'd like to do that,' I said, 'but your husband's special kindness to me looks too suspicious and I don't like it.'

'Yes, that's what I like about you: your good behavior and good manners. I see everything, my dear. You saw my apartment and the unnatural life I lead, eating at the shop and not at home. Our shop is doing well. It's located on the way to the railway station. I can't hire anyone, not because I can't afford to but because of my husband. I've tried a few times. I even ran away from him once; I spent two years in Sicily working as a waitress but it was too hard for me. I hate Sicily, the dirt there. My husband found out where I was and came to take me back. I hardly found any of our furniture. The few things that were left were broken. The girl who had been living with him had left him after a short time. Then he had another one but she left him soon, too. He had a miserable life. Eventually he came for me, begging me to come back. He promised to change, but it's no use. He's sick; he has a weakness for other women. I beg of you, don't pay any attention to him. Do it for me. I like you a lot. We could be very close friends.'

I promised her that it would all turn out for the best.

Then Marysia introduced me to the dressmaker, who showed us some magazines and took measurements. As she worked, I thought about Marysia's story. Why did she have to suffer so much? I hated her husband.

I went to the shop every day to help Marysia as much as I could and pass the time. Sometimes she left me alone there and I managed well. Zygmund visited several times. I felt sorry for him; he was so lonely. He told me that he had written a letter to Parma. Marysia went to the investigation officer and signed an application to assume responsibility for me. The matter took time because she could only remove me from the convent after the application was approved by Rome.

One Sunday, the four of us – Marysia, Luigi, Zygmund, and I – went out together. The next day, Marysia told me that Luigi was furious because I had spent the whole time with Zygmund rather than with him. She smiled as she said it and asked me to be nice to her husband. I promised to try.

One day, as we sat in the back room eating lunch, we heard somebody enter the shop. A second later, Luigi called me over and asked if I knew the man standing near him. He had been in Lwów with the army. I looked at him apprehensively. I shook my head, went back to the back room, and told Marysia that I didn't know the man. Luigi and the stranger left the shop together. I was afraid and agitated now; my heart

119

pounded wildly. Five minutes later, Luigi returned and said, 'That sergeant knows you. He said you're a Jew and you worked for the Italians. He even asked me to be good to you because you went through so much.' I forced myself to smile and told him that I had never seen the man in my life; he must have mistaken me for someone else. Marysia stood next to me and said I was right. She could tell by my nose that I wasn't Jewish.

The incident saddened me terribly. Back in my room at the convent, as I lay on my bed, I thought of my fate. How much longer would I have to struggle? When would I finally be able to be myself? When could I be Klara again and not have to lie? I wanted to be honest with myself and others.

Maria came in, interrupting my thoughts. She told me to go downstairs because a soldier was standing at the gate and asking for Klara. I rushed to the gate, sure that the visitor was one of 'my' soldiers, because only they knew me as Klara rather than Kasia. To my surprise, the man at the gate turned out to be a stranger, a tall, uniformed soldier. I looked at him curiously, hesitant to approach him. Noticing this, he said, 'I'm a friend of Fosco's. I'm staying here in Udine. I got a letter from Fosco this week. He asked me to visit you and to give you 50 lire for your initial needs. I looked for you in the hospital and asked for Klara. Nobody knew a girl by that name, but they sent me here.' He gave me the money and told me that Fosco had finished his furlough and was back in the camp in Parma. His sister would come to take me to their home.

I was thrilled. No longer would I have to live under a false name. At last I could be myself. I thanked the soldier heartily and returned to my room. I kept the news to myself.

The next day, I told Marysia that I would probably be going to Parma to visit a friend from Lwów – the one who had originally advised me to come to Italy. He was now inviting me to stay with his family. Marysia didn't like the idea and tried to talk me out of it. Zygmund visited me that afternoon and walked me back to the convent. I told him what had happened and gave him some of the money that I had received. I thought of him as a brother. He was lonesome. Before we parted, he asked me to remember him or perhaps, later, to invite him to join me in my new place. I promised, although I didn't know myself where I would be or how my new hosts would help me.

When I came back from the shop three days later, I was told that someone had asked for me and would return later. I waited impatiently.

I had been in Udine for three months by then. A few of the Russian girls, especially those who were married or engaged to Italian soldiers, had already left the convent. I was in a rut. I didn't like the town or the kind of life that I had there. In the meantime, however, I had become fluent in Italian. I thought about Fosco's sister. What did she look like? I ate my supper quickly and continued to wait impatiently for the caller. Finally the nun called me to come downstairs. A slender, pretty brunette who looked a lot like Fosco was waiting for me together with the soldier who had visited me before. He introduced the girl to me as Fosco's sister Tina. Then he left. Tina told me that she had booked a room in the local hotel and had come to take me to their home. I couldn't leave without permission from the investigation officer, I explained. Before I could go to see him, however, I had to go to Marysia's shop, since I had promised to be there early and stay until Luigi came with the fruit. Therefore, Tina and I agreed to meet at the shop.

Tina came by at the appointed time and waited with me until Marysia arrived at eleven o'clock. I introduced her to Tina and then introduced Luigi when he came in. 'If you've came to take Kasia away from us,' Luigi said, 'it'll be a shame. We like her as though she were our own sister.' Tina said nothing. She already knew the whole story; while we were alone in the store earlier, I had told her that Marysia and her husband wanted me in their custody and had told the police as much. We said goodbye and went to the investigation office. There, the clerk told Tina that she would have to wait for an answer from Rome. She tried to explain that she had come from Parma especially to take me with her, but the clerk insisted: he could do nothing without permission from Rome. I accompanied Tina to her hotel room. While we were eating lunch, we heard someone yelling that the Germans had taken over Italy. People ran into the streets in panic. Soldiers rushed to buy civilian suits, lest the Wehrmacht take them prisoner. Those who could not obtain civilian clothing in the stores went to private homes to ask for it.

Tina decided to go home instead of waiting for me. If the trains stopped running, she said, she would be stuck in Udine with no money. She told me to go to Parma as soon as I had permission.

I went back to my room in the convent, wondering what to do now. Some time later, the nun at the gate came upstairs to call me. Someone was waiting for me at the gate. It was Luigi. He had come to take me to his home for the night. I packed everything in my valise and went with him.

The radio and newspapers reported the latest news. People were apprehensive and uncertain. They asked each other for their opinions. Everyone was afraid of the Germans, remembering them from the First World War and their history classes. Now an additional piece of news – or was it just a rumor? – circulated by word of mouth: the Germans had abandoned their Italian allies behind the front lines as they retreated in Russia. My thoughts, however, were elsewhere. Above all, I had to escape.

When we got to Luigi's house, Marysia, who had been waiting for us there, said, 'Whatever happens, we'll be together.' I demurred, telling her that I wanted to go to Parma. I had to go there. They couldn't understand why. I understood their point of view. They were such good people; they had offered me their home and I had turned them down. Marysia tried to convince me that I had to stay with them. The trains would stop running regularly; the trip wouldn't be safe. At least, I should wait. I decided to go anyway. I explained to her that in my story to the investigation officer, I had said that I had escaped from the Germans because they had sent us to forced labor in Germany. If the Germans laid hands on the police records now, they would arrest me immediately. Marysia and Luigi weren't convinced.

The next day, I said goodbye to the two of them and promised to return after the war was over. They tried to stop me again, to no avail. I picked up my valise, packed some fruit that they gave me, and headed for the nearest train station.

The station was packed with people, mostly men, who were desperate to escape with the soldiers. Some wore women's blouses instead of men's shirts – anything so as not to be seen in uniform. I circulated among the groups of men, eavesdropping on their conversations. Mostly, they were sharing rumors. I found out when the next train for Bologna was supposed to leave, but some people said it was impossible to reach Bologna. Others said that the train would be rerouted and that the Germans were removing male passengers at the stations to take them to prison camps.

The train arrived at long last. I was shoved into one of the cars along with a crush of people. No one wanted to be left behind. The seats were all taken. I looked around for another woman to keep me company. I spotted one at the far end of the car – the only woman in sight – and went over to her side. Before the train started moving, Fascist police and Germans boarded our car together and ordered all soldiers to get off. Some obeyed; others didn't budge. When the police and the Germans went to the next car, the passengers who had deboarded came back. There was no order at all. The cars were so crowded that the German soldiers didn't even want to re-inspect them thoroughly. They just peered in and walked away.

We were all glad when the train started moving. I decided not to talk to anyone because my Italian might sound suspicious. We traveled all day, making only a few stops. At each station, it was the same as in Udine. A German soldier came onto the train with a policeman and ordered the Italian soldiers to get off. Our car was so crowded that they could not even come in to check. I was glad because nobody paid any attention to me. At one station, we had to change trains. This time, I had a seat on a bench between two men. A woman sat across from me, but the rest of the people were men.

I didn't know exactly where the train was heading, so I asked a man sitting near me how to get to Parma. He told me to get off at the next station and take another train that would leave the next day. He would be doing the same, he said; he was going to visit his brother and invited me to join him. Although he seemed kind and his advice sounded good, I hesitated. Where would I spend the night? I looked up and glanced at the woman opposite me, who sent me a message with her eyes. I understood that the man had misinformed me. She made no further attempt to communicate with me. The man continued to urge me to come with him; later he became insistent. Finally, I told him that I would get off with all the others. That much was true; I would not get off in a strange place by myself. He promised to help me with anything I might need. When we pulled into the next station, he asked me one last time, 'Will you go with me?' 'No,' I said firmly.

After he got off, the woman moved over to sit next to me. She told me that she had heard my questions and his answers. I shouldn't have believed him, she said. He was up to no good and looked suspicious. Then she gave me directions: continue to Bologna and change trains there for Parma. She added that she was also changing trains in Bologna. She would stay with me until the end of that leg of the journey.

Half an hour after midnight, the train stopped. We were told that we had to get off; the train was not going any farther. We were about nine miles from Bologna, it turned out. I climbed down with everyone else and found myself in a field with several buildings nearby. We were told to stay where we were until morning and only then move on toward Bologna. People sat or lay on the grass. Those who had blankets spread them out and tried to make themselves comfortable. The Germans, we heard, were on their way to Bologna to arrest all the men. The other woman and I went over to the houses to sit down. We spotted only two more women in the crowd. I took my coat out of the valise and sat on it. I was tired, hungry, and dirty.

People peered at us through some of the windows. Several young fellows in the crowd asked them for shirts, trousers, or anything else that would make them look like civilians. In response, they said they had already given away everything they could spare. Two soldiers in the crowd stood there begging for whatever they could give. They were a pitiful sight. It hurt me to hear them; their faces reminded me of the beggars in the ghetto ... and of my brothers. I offered them my blouses and rummaged through my valise for anything else that might be suitable. Although I didn't find anything, they noticed how much I wanted to help them and asked where I was going. 'Parma,' I replied.

'That's good,' one of them said. 'We're going to Ferrera. Our train leaves from the same station as yours. Let's go together. You'll help us get past the German posts at the entrance to Bologna. We'll look more like civilians if there's a woman with us.' They removed their military caps and coats. We sat together and talked about past events. One of them told me that the Germans had sent a child to one army camp to order the Italian soldiers to surrender. The soldiers came out and surrendered with their hands up.

Early the next morning, the young men prepared a breakfast of bread and sardines and shared it with me. Then we picked up our things and started walking. There was a long line of people in front of us and behind us. It was a long way to Bologna. We stopped only once, at a well where we could drink and wash up.

I was so weak and exhausted that I could hardly keep going. I had to stop frequently to rest. The young men helped me a lot. One of them carried my valise, but even that was of little use. Finally, I told them to go on by themselves; I would stay where I was for a while and then make my way slowly. They rejected this solution: why stop now, they said, with only one mile left? When we had covered that mile and I asked how much farther we had to go, they said that their previous estimate had been wrong. It couldn't be more than a mile from where we were now. They carried on this way whenever I had to stop to rest. Eventually they had to drag me because I couldn't move; my feet were swollen from the strain and heat. We marched in this fashion for five hours and then spent a sleepless night. I felt terrible about it.

We reached the German checkpoint at the entrance to Bologna at noon the next day. The Germans allowed us to pass unimpeded; they just stared at the wretched souls who had no idea where to go. The train station was still far away, but the hiking was easier now because we were walking on paved surfaces rather than a sandy trail. Throngs of people were heading in the same direction.

When we reached the station, I said goodbye to my new friends. One of them hoped to meet again after the war and gave me his address. I went into the station and asked an employee when the train for Parma would leave. In an hour, the man answered and pointed to the platform. I bought a ticket and found a bench to sit on. What a relief it was to sit down. Somebody sat down next to me and I asked him how long the trip to Parma would take. Not long, he answered: about two hours. I thanked him. Parma really wasn't far away after all, I thought.

Trains heading for different destinations came and went. The station was terribly crowded. At last, I heard a voice calling, 'Parma in another few minutes.' I hurried into a car and took a window seat; I always liked to watch the fields as we passed. The train moved quickly and stopped at only a few stations. Some people got off; others got on. I didn't talk to anyone on the way. I felt an existential emptiness. What now? I asked myself. Parma's coming up, I heard someone say. I picked up my valise and hopped off as soon as the train stopped. I was joined at the station by other passengers who had detrained there. Some of them had relatives waiting for them. Others ordered taxis to take them to their destinations. I went over to a boy in the street and asked him how to get to

Via 22 Giugno. He tried to explain but eventually decided to escort me himself. It was only a few blocks away. When we reached the street, I thanked him and looked for the house number. I found it, went into the building, and walked down a long corridor, checking each door for the name. Just then, a door opened. A girl stepped into the corridor and asked me if I was looking for Fosco's family. 'Yes, I am,' I said. She invited me in and said, 'You're Klara, aren't you? I'm Lidia, Fosco's older sister. I recognized you right away. You look exactly as Fosco described you.'

She showed me to another room, where I found Tina sewing. We greeted each other like old friends. Lidia left us to do some shopping. Tina told me to make myself at home and asked me how I had come; they had heard that the train had not reached Bologna. I described my journey briefly and she described hers. Lidia came back and served us drinks. Then I asked where Fosco was. The sisters looked at each other sadly and said that he had been taken prisoner. The Germans had surrounded their camp. Now they were behind a fence in a small park. They could walk around; we would see him later. I felt bad. Such a possibility had never occurred to me.

That evening, I met Fosco's brother Vittorio. The oldest member of the household, he also turned out to be the head of the household and a very nice person who took care of everything and knew everything. The siblings conversed with each other in a dialect that I didn't understand, but Vittorio told me in standard Italian not to worry about a thing. They would take care of any matter that came up.

The next day before noon, Tina took me to the park. On the way, she told me how nice that part of town was, with its swimming pool and recreation buildings. The prisoners were being housed in those buildings right now. Nobody knew what the Germans intended to do with them. Would they be taken to Germany? Some said they had been arrested only to prevent a revolt. As soon as the Germans could install a new government that would do their bidding, they would let the soldiers return to their camps.

When we reached the park gate, Tina called over one of the soldiers and asked him to call Fosco. Fosco came to the fence a few minutes later. He was delighted to see me and asked how I was feeling and how I liked Parma. He warned me to stay at home and not to speak to anyone I didn't know, lest I be recognized as a stranger. Now Fosco and his sister lapsed into the dialect that I didn't understand. Later, we said goodbye and went home, where we found Lidia working in the small room.

The apartment was old and had no modern comforts. We washed in a bowl of water in the kitchen. The lavatory was in a narrow hallway. The stove was heated with wooden coals and the flame was hard to fan until it grew to its full height. In the kitchen was a large dining table. The next room was a bedroom with two beds and a mirror. Adjacent to it was the small room where Tina worked; it was furnished with a sofa and a desk. Vittorio held a white-collar job and his earnings and Tina's went for household needs. The family was poor, but their harmony and kind-heartedness gave me a good feeling about my decision to join them.

I noticed that they didn't have enough food. Everything was rationed on the basis of personal cards. Bread, the main staple, was baked in the form of rolls, and each person received one and a half a day. Soup, meat, and everything else was similarly doled out. I realized that anything I ate was taken away from my hosts. They treated me as well as they could. Vittorio took me to the theater; Tina showed me the town and its surroundings.

One evening, Vittorio came home with his girlfriend, a nice, pretty girl named Anna, and introduced me to her. As we chatted, Anna asked me how I liked it there and engaged in similar small talk. After she left, Tina described the troubles that Anna had gone through. Her father was a newspaper correspondent. An anti-Fascist, he had written an article against the Fascist regime and had been arrested and sent to Africa. Anna had not seen him in years. Now, he had managed to escape and was hiding at home under a false name. The whole family feared for his safety. Ah, tragedies everywhere!

Anna came by the next day and brought me three pairs of underwear. 'They're for you,' she said. I knew how hard it was to obtain underwear; she had probably bought them on the black market. I thanked her and said that I would like to get her a fine wedding gift. 'Gifts are not given in order to get something in exchange,' she said.

The next day, I met one of my hosts' neighbors, Lucia, and her husband Decimo. Why Decimo? I wondered. Lucia explained that all the children in his family had been given numbers instead of names: Primo, Secondo, etc. He was the tenth child in the family. I conversed with them and found them to be nice and kind. In fact, after so much suffering, I now took a liking to anyone who greeted me with a smile.

A few days later, Lidia and Tina told me that Fosco had escaped from the prison camp and had gone into hiding with some friends. Don't tell anyone, they warned me. They were about to go with him to the hills; I would be alone for a few days, since Vittorio worked in a village and came home only once a week, but a friend of theirs, Gina, would come to keep me company at night. I was elated to hear that Fosco was free. I would feel even safer if he were here. And I asked no questions about his hide-out.

Tina and Lidia left that afternoon. Alone in the house, I looked over their family pictures. Then I heard somebody calling from outside. I went to the window and saw Fosco with his sisters. He had come to say goodbye to me before leaving for the hills. It was so sweet of him. Standing in the yard near the window, he warned me not to come out and told me to take care of myself. He'd be back soon, he promised. I wished him the best of luck. He left and I went back to looking at the pictures.

Later, I visited Lucia. A close friend of the family, she told me about Fosco and his mother. Although I didn't bring up the subject, she told me that his mother liked to drink alcoholic beverages. The children had sent her to a place called Fontenelate, where she had two unmarried sisters, both of whom were poor. Does tragedy leave its mark in every house? I asked myself. As I sat with Lucia, she continued to divulge the family's most intimate stories. From my standpoint, these were the kindest and nicest people on earth. All I was curious about was how they had reached this place.

Gina came over in the evening with a gift of lipstick. We lay on the beds and talked for a long time. At last, she told me that she was Fosco's girlfriend. They had begun to date before he was sent to the front. While he was away from Italy, they had written to each other very often. 'I waited for him all the time. I didn't go out with other boys,' she said and started to cry. I realized that she thought I was Fosco's girlfriend. I was at a loss for words because I had no idea what Fosco's sister had said about me. Blandly I assured her that nothing had changed. Gina went home in the morning, leaving me alone again. I wondered what to do next; I couldn't stay with these people and do nothing.

Tina and Lidia returned that evening. I was very glad to see them. Everything had worked out well, they said. Fosco was in a safe place.

8 The Convent

One day, Tina told me that their priest, Padre Francesco, had promised to find me a place in a convent. The very next day, Padre Francesco told Tina and Lidia that he could take me to a convent in Traversetolo. He asked if I could mend stockings or cook and help out in the kitchen. He drew up a list of things that I should bring, such as long-sleeved underwear and modest nightgowns.

Tina took me to a woman she knew, a very religious spinster who lived on the second floor of a building not far away. When the woman opened the door and invited us in, Tina introduced me and explained the purpose of our visit: I was going to attend school at the Convent of Traversetolo and must have special underwear. Would she be willing to give me some things she didn't need? She was glad to comply; she had attended the same school when she was young and still felt warmly about the convent. She took out some shirts with long sleeves and high necklines. As she packed them and some other things, she told me about the convent and religious matters. Finally, she promised to visit me. We thanked her for everything, bade her goodbye, and left. Everything was ready for Sunday, when I would travel to the convent.

I had mixed feelings about the move. I was pleased to stop being a burden on these nice people, but I hated to leave them to go to a new place again. Vittorio and Tina decided to escort me to Traversetolo by bicycle because I couldn't take the bus without a special permit from the police. I didn't know how far it was. I was eager to get the trip over with and no longer have to be afraid and run from place to place. Tina placed my valise on her bicycle and Vittorio invited me to ride with him on his. It was a difficult uphill ride. We stopped several times to rest. Tina and Vittorio changed bicycles and burdens three or four times, stopping in between to rest. After two and a half hours of travel, we reached the small town of Traversetolo and stopped in the main piazza where stores, restaurants, and the bus terminal were located.

Vittorio invited us to a small restaurant for lunch, and Vittorio ordered roast beef with potatoes. The restaurateur asked for our ration cards, without which we couldn't order a thing. While we were there, Vittorio asked where the convent was and was told that it was nearby. We headed there after lunch.

My heart pounded as we approached the building. I had no idea what awaited me there. As Tina tugged on the bell at the entrance gate, I studied the impressive two-story structure. The first-floor façade was windowless, and most of the windows on the second floor were shuttered. The lower halves of the few open windows were covered with white curtains. In the center of the building was a heavy gate with a small window through which one of the nuns, stationed at the gate, could see who was there.

An elderly, hunchbacked nun opened the gate. Tina and Vittorio asked for the Mother Superior. The old nun pulled a cord and allowed the bell to ring once – a signal to the Mother Superior that she was wanted at the gate. We were led to a *parlatorio*, a guest room of sorts, where we sat and waited. Vittorio and Tina tried to comfort me by saying that my stay at the convent would be temporary. The war would be over soon, they continued hopefully, but for now this was the safest place for me.

A tall, middle-aged woman entered the room and greeted us: 'Sia lodato Gesu' Cristo.'

'Sempre Sia lodato,' Tina and Vittorio replied.

The Mother Superior was dressed in black except for a starched white cap under which her hair was pinned tightly. A large crucifix dangled from her neck, and a rosary with a small crucifix was suspended from the right side of her dress.

She had been expecting me. She asked me how fluent my Italian was and what I was capable of doing. I could sew, I said, and I could help out in the kitchen. Then she asked me whether I had clothing that conformed with the rules of the convent. Yes, Tina answered in my stead, and they would send me anything else that I might need. The Mother Superior said that I would be helping out with all kinds of work; this would give me experience for later in my life, when I would have to fend for myself.

Now she turned to Tina and Vittorio and asked them about their lives, what they did, how they managed with the food in their town, and so on. Then she asked them for the latest news and they talked politics and shared their thoughts about the war. When would it end? she asked them. If people had stronger faith in God, she declared, there would be no wars. 'We always pray for the soldiers who do the fighting and for ordinary people and ask that God forgive them.' Then the Mother Superior invited us to the chapel. We followed her down a long hallway, at the end of which she opened a door to a large room. There were three rows of benches in the middle of the room. The left-hand wall was embellished with a fine, large altar and some beautiful paintings, all of which looked new. The other walls were decorated with paintings of the Via Dolorosa. We knelt and the Mother Superior recited the Ave Maria. Tina and Vittorio recited the second part of the prayer.

When they finished their devotions, we went out to the yard. The Mother Superior told us that the chapel was newly built and showed us other parts of the convent that were also of recent construction. A wide gate opened onto fields belonging to the convent. I listened to and looked at everything. I thought I would like this place since it was so firmly planted in nature. Vittorio and Tina were also pleasantly surprised by its loveliness.

We returned to the *parlatorio*. Tina and Vittorio decided to go home. They had a long trip ahead of them and their time was limited, since there was a curfew for civilians on the main roads. It was very hard for me to part with these good people. Seeing the sad look on my face, they said, 'Don't worry. We'll visit you often.' I escorted them to the gate and said my farewells. My heart ached as the gate closed behind them.

The Mother Superior told me to take my belongings and come to her office. She wanted to speak with me. Her office, a small room on the first floor, was furnished sparsely with a couch, a desk, two chairs, and pictures of saints on the walls. She seated herself behind the desk and invited me to pull the other chair near hers. She studied me critically and then asked, 'Who told you to do this?' Uncomprehending, I stared at her like a frightened child. 'Take off that figurine,' she said. 'It's disrespectful to hang it with the Holy Mary.' Suddenly I realized what she meant. On my necklace, the likeness of Mary was hanging with the miniature hunchback figurine that Mario had given me back in Poland as a lucky charm. The Mother Superior then added, 'You should not believe in anything other than Jesus Christ.' I removed the hunchback but told her that I wanted to keep it because it was a souvenir from a man who done so much to help me survive. I put it in my pocket.

The Mother Superior explained that the people in the convent – children aged eight to 15 – should not know about my origins. Disclosure would be unsafe for me and for them. 'Because of your accent, we'll tell them you're from Bolzano, a border town. Your parents were killed when the town was bombed.' She continued, 'I'll have to register you with the local council as a new arrival and get you ration cards. You'll have to change your name for safety's sake. We'll call you Clara Morselli. What do you think?' I liked it. We decided to visit the council the next day. She gave me a prayer book, instructed me to memorize the Pater Noster and the Ave Maria, and told me, 'After a few days, we'll prepare you for baptism. You'll take on our religion and your soul will be saved.'

She escorted me out of her office and told me to take my valise to the second floor. There, she led me to one of the beds in a large bedroom. 'This will be your bed and here's a chest of drawers for your clothes.' I thanked her; then she walked out. Alone in the room, I had my first chance to digest everything she had told me. For reasons I could not fathom, I did not like the way she had spoken to me. She was too strict and official. As I arranged my clothes in the drawers, I heard a bell ringing. A nun passing by told me to go down to the main dining room; it was suppertime. I thanked her and headed in the direction of the voices.

A bit scared and shy, I went to the dining room and stood in the doorway. Inside, I saw two rows of young girls and a nun. They clasped their hands in prayer before seating themselves at the table. As I waited for them to finish the prayer, they all turned in my direction and stared. A nun came over to me, invited me to enter, and showed me to a place at the head of the table. She probably knew about me, I thought, because she didn't ask any questions. She accepted me with a smile – just the thing that I missed and needed so much. I was given two dishes, a set of silverware, and a napkin. She explained to me that after I finished eating I would have to wash the dishes and place them in a drawer at my place at the table. Everyone had such a drawer. 'Si Signora, grazie,' I answered.

Everybody in the dining room ate silently. One of the girls read a story about a saint. Later, she was relieved by another girl, who continued reading while the first one ate. Anyone who wanted more food raised her hand and the nun came over and served her what she wanted. The nun's name, I learned, was Sr (Sister) M. Gertrude. After supper, the children stood up to recite the Grace after Meals. Then we all left the dining room.

Two girls stayed behind as dining room orderlies. Two other girls went into the kitchen to wash the kitchen utensils. All the rest went to the yard to play, under the supervision of Sr M. Gertrude. 'What I should do now?' I asked Sr M. Gertrude. She told me to go to the kitchen and put all the washed utensils away. 'Si, Signora,' I said. I did as I was told.

The kitchen was spacious. Against one wall was a large, coal-fired iron oven. Along the opposite wall was a work table. On the left side of the table were gas burners. Two nuns were working in the kitchen when I came in.

'Sr M. Gertrude sent me in to help you,' I said.

'Are you new here?' one of them asked.

'Si, Signora.'

'We're glad to have you,' said the younger one.

'What can I help you with?' I asked. She directed me to a small room that she called the *vasellame*, a special place for washing dishes. My job was to take the utensils that the two girls had washed back to the kitchen and hang them on hooks along the walls.

While I worked, I learned the nuns' names. The younger one was Sr Angela; the older one was Sr Agata. Sr Angela was very pretty, with big blue eyes, white teeth, a good complexion, and a sweet smile. I wondered why a lovely young girl like that would sequester herself in a convent and disengage from the rest of the world. Later, the two nuns went out and another girl came in to scrub the floors. The nuns had gone off to say their prayers, she told me. After finishing my work, I reported to Sr M. Gertrude, who was still watching the girls in the playground. She told me that she had heard I was handy in sewing and mending. She was willing to put me to work as her helper with those chores. 'Grazie,' I answered.

At eight o'clock that evening, we all went to the chapel for vespers. Afterwards, we left the chapel in pairs to go to the bedroom, accompanied by Sr M. Gertrude. The bedroom was spacious indeed. It was furnished with three rows of beds. The nuns' beds stood in the corners and were separated from the rest of the room by movable partitions. The girls put on their nightgowns and knelt near their beds for compline. I did the same. When we were all in bed, Sr M. Gertrude shut off the lights and left. The girl in the next bed whispered to me that the nun had gone out to say her own evening prayers.

I tossed in bed sleeplessly. I had many questions about the new place but no one to ask. It was very quiet in the room; all

I could hear was the breathing of the sleeping girls. Later, I saw the nuns returning from their prayers. They moved quietly in the dark. Their shadows frightened me. One of the nuns approached my bed and made the sign of the cross over my face. I felt drops of water on my face. She had probably brought holy water from the chapel. Then I recognized her; it was Sr M. Gertrude. Still unable to sleep, I thought about her. I liked her because of her sincerity toward me and felt that I had found in her a good friend.

The next morning, a nun entered the bedroom at seven o'clock and clapped her hands to wake us. Simultaneously, bells rang. The girls leaped out of bed and removed their nightgowns. Under them, they had underwear. Then they put on their robes and went to a washroom with sinks and taps along one wall and hooks along the opposite wall, on which they hung their towels and a bag containing soap and a toothbrush. After washing, we all returned to the bedroom to finish dressing and went down to the chapel for morning prayers.

There were several nuns in the chapel; they occupied rows on the left-hand side. In the middle rows were a few older people from the village who came for the half-hour morning service. A nun led us to the right-hand rows. Two nuns knelt with us and took care of us. When we finished, we went to the dining room. The bells rang for breakfast. Another nun, the same one who had awakened us that morning, was in the dining room that day. Sr Celina was her name. A short, dark, very pleasant-looking woman, she recited the Grace before Meals and then served coffee and one roll to each of us.

After breakfast, we said Grace, washed our cups, and returned to the bedroom to make our beds. Again two orderlies remained behind to clean the whole bedroom; the others headed for the classrooms. Lessons started at nine. I went to the kitchen to peel potatoes, slice them very thin, and grate cheese for *formaggio parmigiano*.

In the kitchen I met an older woman named Gemma, who had a hunchback, and a girl named Anita who was scrubbing the floor. Sr Angela had told me about Gemma and said she was a saint. Gemma's mother had been a servant at the convent. Gemma herself had wanted to be a nun, but nuns in a convent do only the hardest jobs and live under very difficult conditions. Because of her poor health, she was not accepted. Just the same, she decided to stay in the convent as a servant. When I met her, she was working in the chicken coops, feeding the chickens and collecting the eggs. She had spent her entire life in the convent and did any job that had to be done. I listened to everyone's stories about everything and everyone. It was all new to me. In fact, I had wondered about the lives of convent nuns ever since I had observed them as a child in Lwów.

Gemma asked me if I would like to see her chickens. She led me out of the kitchen to a fenced yard and showed me the fowl, especially the little chicks that she liked so much. She also had a big brown cat that accompanied her wherever she went. She raised roosters that she castrated in a very primitive way. Nearby, I also saw rabbits in cages; Anita was in charge of these. Every afternoon Anita would go out to the field and cut grass for the rabbits. She also took one of the bunnies out of his cage and played with him. She wanted to hand him to me, so that I could hold him and see how nice and soft he was. I was afraid to touch him and hold him by his ears as she did. She had 60 rabbits, she said, and she would have had more had she not given some of them to the kitchen to be cooked. I simply could not understand why these poor creatures should be killed. 'I won't eat them,' I said loudly. The thought of 'killing' reminded me of those innocent, defenseless people whom the Germans had killed so barbarically.

Later, Anita showed me another project of hers, a pigsty where she raised two big hogs on kitchen leftovers and other food. The Mother Superior had brought them in when they were very small, she explained. She had been raising them all year and before Christmas they would be slaughtered by two men who were experts at that job. They would make the swine into products that could be stored and used all year round – sausages, lard, and several kinds of salami. This was all a big novelty to me; I had grown up in a large city and had never seen such an enterprise before. The bell rang and Anita told me it was lunchtime.

By now I realized that time in the convent was told by bells, from early morning until bedtime. Bells rang for the first prayers, for breakfast, at 9.00 a.m. for the beginning of classes, at noon for lunch, at 3.00 p.m. for school again, at 4.30 p.m. for rosary prayers, at five for supper, and at eight for vespers. Bells were also used to summon the nuns, each of whom had a number. The Mother Superior was called by one ring, for example, and Sr M. Gertrude by two rings.

We returned to the kitchen and helped carry the food into the dining room. All the girls were seated at the tables; Sr Celina was with them. We took our places for lunch. After lunch, I went back to work. In the afternoon, when I had finished, I took my prayer book and went to the fields to memorize the prayers. On the *careggiata* (a path in the middle of the field), I encountered an attractive nun who approached me with a pleasant smile and asked, 'How do you like it here, Clara?' I was surprised that she knew my name. She told me that Padre Francesco, her confessor, had told her all about me. 'My name is Sr Gabriela. I've come here for a six-day vacation. I'm a teacher at the Collegio in Parma, and when Padre Francesco came here to see the Mother Superior about you, he visited me as well and told me about you.' On our way back to the convent, she told me that two of her brothers were with the army in Poland.

I saw Sr M. Gertrude on the balcony and walked with her to her workroom. I told her I had met Sr Gabriela. She said she knew that Sr Gabriela had met with Padre Francesco but, in her opinion, he was too softhearted toward her. I didn't understand what she meant by that but I sensed that something was wrong. The next day, I noticed that Sr Gabriela was alone most of the time; no one spoke with her. Two days later, she returned to Parma. There were rumors among the girls in our convent that Sr Gabriela was planning to leave her convent in Parma. I found this very interesting and wanted to know what her motives might be.

On my seventh day in the convent, the Mother Superior summoned me to her office and ordered me to take my clothes from the bedroom and move to another room. I did as I was told and was ushered to a small room with only two beds. 'You will sleep here temporarily,' the Mother Superior explained. 'The Monsignor will come early in the morning before the first prayers to christen you.' She went out and left me alone in the room. Sr Gertrude came in, helped me to make my bed, and told me not to worry. She would visit the next morning to wake me up and accompany me. I thanked her and she left. I was glad to be alone; I didn't feel like talking to anyone just then.

I felt terribly agitated and lonely all night. I thought about my entire family having been killed. I cried and may have fallen asleep briefly. Very early in the morning, Sr M. Gertrude woke me up. We went together to the chapel. There, she placed a white veil on my head. I stepped up to the altar, where the Monsignor and the Mother Superior were waiting. The Monsignor opened a book and recited some prayers. In several places, I had to reply 'Rinuncio' (I renounce) and the Monsignor made the sign of the cross on my forehead and behind my ears. He named me Maria Angela. From then on, I was allowed to take communion.

After the christening ceremony, I remained in the chapel, kneeling. The bell rang and the girls came into the chapel, visibly surprised to find me there. They whispered to one another. I suspected they were talking about me, but I didn't know what they were saying. After the prayers, on our way to the dining room, one of the older girls, Anna, approached me and said to me, 'Don't be a nun. It's not the life for you. If you have nowhere to go or no one to go to, I'll take you to my home. My parents are good people. I'll write to them and they'll be glad to have you. I'm sure of it.' I thanked her and told her not to worry about me. Then Sr Celina came over and we had to stop talking. Now I knew what they had been whispering about and why they were always looking at me so strangely.

When I went to the kitchen after breakfast, the nuns there had a surprise for me. They had baked a special cake for the occasion of my christening. Sr Angela handed it to me and said, 'If you were to die today, you'd be a saint. Your soul would go directly to Paradise because you are free of sin. You have been reborn.'

'I hope I won't die today,' I said. 'I feel just fine.' I went upstairs and found Sr M. Gertrude in her workroom near the window, knitting gloves. I sat down near her and asked her about the christening ceremony. What did making the sign of the cross with holy water on my forehead mean?

'You see,' Sr M. Gertrude said, 'everyone is born with the sin of Adam and Eve. The holy water cleanses you and renders you pure to serve God. Later, you have to see your priest and confess your sins before him. He can help you to be forgiven. He is the minister presented to you by the will of God.'

I liked Sr M. Gertrude and enjoyed talking with her. I would finish my work in the kitchen as quickly as possible in order to be with her. Then I would help her with her own work and we would talk.

Girls from the nearby village also visited the convent school. One of them was 16-year-old Maria, who kept Sr M. Gertrude informed of the latest news that she had heard on the radio or read in the papers. Sr M. Gertrude introduced me to Maria and we became good friends. Maria went with me to a photographer to take pictures for a new I.D. card, issued to me by the local council in the name of Clara Morselli. I then received ration cards and was indistinguishable from everyone else in the convent.

December came around. The girls were excited about going home for Christmas vacation. I didn't know yet how I would spend Christmas. I was surprised one day when the Mother Superior handed me a letter from Fosco's family inviting me to their home for Christmas. Happily, I showed the letter to Sr

M. Gertrude. She was pleased, too, and reminded me to visit Padre Francesco while I was there. Impatiently, I waited for the day.

I went by bus this time. They were expecting me. I was pleasantly surprised to find Fosco there as well. He had returned from the hills several days earlier. The whole family was seated around the table. They had another surprise for me: a silver bracelet with a likeness of the Virgin Mary. A date was engraved on the back: November 23, 1943, the date of my christening. Tina told me that the likeness came from the village of Fontanella, where Mary had once appeared to the population in a vision. Since then, people would go there annually on pilgrimage.

I had a very nice time with them. They took me to the theater and for walks to meet their relatives. I spent my free time with Tina in her workroom, knitting a sweater as we chatted. She told me about her boyfriend, whom I later met in their home. The week flew by and soon I had to return to the convent.

The monotony of my daily life resumed. Again I wore my black dress with the white collar; again I did the same work, first in the kitchen and afterwards with Sr M. Gertrude. I often went to my darkened room, leaned against the heating pipes, and cried. At those times I wanted to stay out of sight and be alone with my thoughts. It was no use; Sr M. Gertrude always found me there. I did feel that she was a close friend who understood me well. I liked telling her about my family, but sometimes I just sat with her and cried. She didn't stop me, since she knew that my tears made me feel better for a while. She comforted me by promising that God would see my suffering and help me. Twice a week, I got up very early and helped her make bread by kneading the dough with a *gramola*, a simple wooden roller.

One day, the Mother Superior asked me to accompany her to town. The rule in the convent was that a nun should never go out by herself. We went by bus. Along the way, she recited the Ave Maria and I followed with the second part. The passengers watched us as we prayed. In town, we visited two convents that were affiliated with our order, the Sacred Heart. The first was an orphanage; it seemed to be very poor in comparison with ours. The other was a school for wealthier girls, a very nice place. There I had a happy encounter with Sr Gabriela, who showed me around after lunch.

In one room was a bed on which Napoleon had slept while in Parma. The nuns were very proud to show it to every visitor. This room was always locked and kept exactly as it had been during Napoleon's time. In the meantime, the Mother Superior had taken care of her affairs. We went to see Padre Francesco, who gave us his blessing. Then we left for home, as I had come to regard our convent.

Winter passed and a pleasant spring followed. The fruit trees in the orchard were blooming and the season was felt everywhere. On Sundays, we went to the church in the village and met various people. The girls were pleased with this arrangement; it was a change for them. They could also look at the young boys and talk about them afterwards. Furthermore, spring was the time for trips to the hills. I liked those trips; we had a lot of fun. More seriously, I marveled at the way the peasants cultivated every bit of ground, even planting grapevines on the hilltops. They turned the soil with a primitive plow pulled by a pair of oxen. Whole families, including children, worked in the fields in the springtime. We visited several villages in the vicinity and stopped to rest at the home of a priest. The priest was usually the most important person in such a village. He was preacher, comforter, and legal advisor. He was consulted on every problem that arose. Young people gathered in his home one or two evenings a week, and he gave them religious instruction and sang religious songs with them. Such was the life of the people who lived in the mountains.

I was on good terms with all the nuns, especially the ones who worked in the kitchen, Sr Angela and Sr Agata. Sometimes I discussed convent life with Sr Angela. She was in the last year of her five-year probationary period, after which she would go to Rome and undergo a ritual engagement to God, conducted by a bishop. She would lie on the floor and be covered with a linen cloth. Candles would be lit at her sides. This would signify her renunciation of life in this world; henceforth her entire life would be pledged to the service of God. The bishop would then read out a list of all the earthly things that she would renounce. She would receive a silver ring engraved with crosses and rename herself after a saint. Life in this world was only temporary, Sr Angela said. In the other world, life is for eternity. It was worth suffering in this world to earn eternal life there. The nun would then be transferred to a different convent, far from her home and family. Years might pass before she saw her family again. She could write letters to her family, but these letters, as well as incoming correspondence, would be censored by the Mother Superior.

I tried unsuccessfully to understand the girls who chose this kind of career. The main reason for their living in the convent, in my opinion, was that they had enrolled when they were very young and inexperienced. Weak of character and afraid to face life in the future, they chose what they considered the path of least resistance.

One afternoon, Anita and I went for a walk along the interior road. She told me about her sorrows and suffering. She had been there for eight years, since the age of six. Her mother had died; her father was in the army. An aunt who was a nun in a convent in Rome had placed her here. No one paid for her board and tuition. Now that her elementary schooling was over, she had to work. She hated the place. She wanted to be like other girls, to have her long hair cut and to wear brightly colored dresses instead of the black ones that she had worn all her life. She dreamed of being with boys. Once she had had an opportunity to take food to the young workers in the field. This had made her extremely happy. She was eager for the war to end; then she would leave the convent and live in a city with her father.

I felt sorry for her. She knew so little about life outside. She had no experience and no one to protect and guide her. She imbibed the stories of other girls who went home for their vacations. They all returned with tales of adventures and dates. Anita saw only the brightness of life on the outside and did not appreciate the sadness. I tried to explain, without discouraging her, that she would do best to stay at the convent until she had more knowledge and experience. Specifically, she should wait until her father came back and had a home ready for her. She turned a deaf ear to my advice. She couldn't stand it anymore, she said; she would leave the place right then if only she could.

The nuns kept the girls on a tight leash. For instance, they never allowed two girls to go to the washroom together; they had to go one by one. If two girls talked among themselves, a nun slipped behind them instantly to eavesdrop. Once, when the girls were already in bed, the nun on duty turned off the light and left the room. Upon hearing the girls talking, she returned and clapped her hands. All the girls had to get up and dress again. The next day, she punished them further by ordering them to write a sentence 50 times. Naturally, the girls resented the strictures and did the opposite of what they were told. The nuns accused Anita of taking part in this uprising. She was a bad influence on them, the nuns said, always talking loudly against the nuns and about leaving the convent.

However, the girls were also at odds with their educators. They were especially cruel to Sr Magdalena, their piano and French teacher. Born in France, Sr Magdalena had been sent to Spain for a couple of years after completing her nun's training and had taught in a convent there. Now she was confused by the Italian language and often inserted foreign words in her lectures. The girls responded with laughter and disruptions.

Most of the girls went home at Easter time; I stayed around. The holiday service included three sets of morning prayers. All that kneeling left my knees sore. After Easter, life in the convent continued in its usual monotonous and clois-tered way. We had no radio or newspapers. Our only sources of news, or rumors, were the students who came from the nearby village.

Meanwhile, SS troops had taken over a two-story building across from the convent. Again I saw the barbaric faces of Germans, this time from my bedroom window. They even entered the convent on several occasions. Italian partisans in the hills would come into the village and harass the Germans, who responded by placing the village under curfew and searching for the partisans in every possible place, including the convent. We stood in the yard watching them probe every corner. I wasn't afraid of them this time, even when they glanced in my direction. They were looking at me as they would look at any woman, I knew. A nun brought them a drink from the kitchen and they left.

Prayer services were conducted by the Monsignor and two priests who came to the convent from the outside. One of the priests was a tall, good-looking man who had a smile and a good word for everyone. His name was Don Emanuel. The girls liked to attend his services because they were very quick. The other priest, Father Augusto, was a skinny man with a bad leg. He was very devoted to his religious duties. During his prayers, he made predictions. This made the service drag on, of course. He also organized a choir and was active with the village youth. The Monsignor was an older man who led the services very slowly. When the girls woke up each morning, they would ask the nun on duty who would be leading the services that day; they were always disappointed when they were told that it would be the Monsignor. For confession, however, they liked the old Monsignor better than the young priests. I was not exempt from confession, although I once tried to explain to Sr Agata that I had no sins to confess since I didn't feel that I had done anything wrong. That's impossible, Sr Agata replied. Even the Virgin Mary committed seven sins, and she was a saint.

By now I had formed an opinion about priests. They were not only God's ministers, I decided; some of them were very clever people who knew a great deal of psychology. They

146

understood people as individuals, had special insights into people's problems, and gave them comfort.

I fell into bleak moods from time to time. The noiselessness of the convent or, sometimes, news about German depredations against the Italian partisans reminded me of what the Germans had done to me and my family back in Poland. In such cases, I could not sleep at night and felt that I had to talk to someone who would understand me. I went to the priest. Once I asked him whether it would not be better for me to join the partisans. Perhaps this would give me relief. The priest said that he understood me very well and then told me a parable. Once there was a canary locked in a cage. Her owner took wonderful care of her, giving her food, water, and love. But the canary was not happy. She wanted to be free. The bird took the first opportunity to fly out of her open cage. She settled on a branch of a tree. A hunter noticed her there and shot her. 'I hope you understand what I mean,' the priest said. Yes, I understood. I thanked him and left. On my way, I reflected on the parable and realized that the priest was right. What he said calmed me for a while.

The priest also had great influence on the nuns, who accepted his views about several problems, one of which was related to me. Sr M. Gertrude always made sure that I had enough to wear. She regularly surprised me with another dress or pair of underwear that she had received from women at the village church. Once, she took me to the attic to inspect some boxes of dresses that were kept there for plays performed at the convent; she thought we might find something suitable there. The problem arose when Sr M. Gertrude received a length of silk from someone and wanted to make me a dress from it. The Mother Superior insisted that the dress be long-sleeved, although the material and the current fashion argued otherwise. Sr M. Gertrude tried to explain this to the Mother Superior, but when she would not authorize a more modern style, Sr M. Gertrude asked the priest for advice. He listened to her carefully and said, 'Maria Angela' – my newly given name – 'should be like all girls her age. Don't overdo it but don't leave her behind the other girls in her style of dress.' His opinion was accepted; Sr M. Gertrude made the dress the way she wanted. Whenever I wore it, the Mother Superior criticized it anyway, saying that it was too short and too tight.

In brief, Sr M. Gertrude acted like a mother to me. Praying was not enough for her; she needed a person to whom she could devote herself. She met this need by taking care of me, and I found in her a real friend.

The Mother Superior was just the opposite. She seemed to miss no opportunity to criticize me. Once she advised me to let my hair grow and braid it as the other girls did. Sr M. Gertrude was against this; she said I should do my hair as I wanted; I was not a child anymore. On other occasions, the Mother Superior spoke critically of the Jewish religion and asked why my parents had not converted to Catholicism. I never answered her. She lacked the tact and understanding to get along with others. I always tried to stay out of her way. When Sr M. Gertrude asked me why, I explained that I disliked the Mother Superior and didn't think someone like her should be the principal of a school. The nuns and the girls didn't like her either, I observed. Sr M. Gertrude explained that she might not really be so bad, just gruff. In fact, Sr M. Gertrude was the only one who stayed on the Mother Superior's good side. She even represented her in the convent during her absences.

The day after my conversation with Sr M. Gertrude, the Mother Superior called me into her office. She urged me to stop avoiding her. She was my good mother, she said, and she wanted me to be happy there. Then she gave me 100 lire and some underwear as presents. I thanked her but said nothing more. Obviously, Sr M. Gertrude had told her everything I had said about her.

The girls went home for summer vacation and were replaced by the orphans and nuns from the convent in Parma. A very obedient and well-behaved bunch, they were of different ages, and I was told that once they turned 18 they would be allowed to leave the convent. They accepted all kinds of work – knitting, sewing, and so on – to cover some of their board and tuition. Various families covered the rest in the form of monthly payments. I liked to spent my free time with these girls, learning useful things about handicrafts from them. The girls, in turn, were happy to be at our place. It was more open than their own convent and they could walk around and play. They stayed with us for two weeks, and we were very sad when they left.

We also hosted three teachers from nearby towns. One of them, Blanche, was only a year or two older than I. Sometimes she stayed with us overnight, and on those evenings when we were together, we learned about each other and became close friends. Once Blanche invited me to her home in Parma for a weekend. She wanted me to meet her family. I obtained permission to take the trip and met her parents and sister, who lived in a fine, large house of their own. We had a lovely time together. They told me that Sr Gabriela had left the convent. She had fallen desperately in love with an army officer who had visited her together with one of her brothers. Her Mother Superior had found out about the relationship by chance. When the mother of one of the girls went to see Sr Gabriela, the Mother Superior took over the class she was teaching and found love letters addressed to Sr Gabriela in the record book. The Mother Superior wanted to forgive her and to help her consign the matter to the past, but Sr Gabriela was too madly in love to change her mind. Instead, she left the convent, a process fraught with difficulties. I obtained her address from Blanche and went to visit her.

I found the place easily and knocked on the door. When she opened it, I was confused for a moment. She had changed drastically. She was delighted to see me and had the same lovely smile and the same eyes, but her beauty was gone and her hair was straggly. She was not the same Sr Gabriela whom I had known. Noticing my surprise, she explained that her hair had been ruined by being covered for so many years, but she hoped it would recover soon. She invited me inside, showed me all the love letters that she had received from her fiancé, and read to me the diary that she been keeping ever since she had fallen in love. I listened eagerly. The look on her face was as innocent as a young girl's, even though she was 30 years old. We talked about the convent and the other nuns. She asked about everyone. I realized that she felt a little guilty. She defended herself, stressing that she went to church every day. She was a good Christian, she said, and she hoped that God had forgiven her. It was late. I took my leave and went back to Blanche, who agreed that Gabriela had changed since she had left the convent.

I returned to my convent after a lovely weekend. I did not tell Sr M. Gertrude about my visit to Gabriela, who had become an off-limits topic since she had left the fold.

Sr Gertrude was waiting eagerly for me with important news. She showed me a picture postcard from a girl in a convent in Bergamo, a village near Milan. The message said that the Virgin Mary had appeared in Bergamo. The girl had been playing with two boys in a field and saw the Virgin on the branches of a tall tree. Mary told the girl that she had come because of the weeping of mothers whose sons were on the battlefield. She would reappear in three weeks' time and would tell them when the war would end. Sr M. Gertrude urged me to go there and make my wish at that holy place. 'You can be sure that your wish will be fulfilled,' she said.

Later, we were informed in a letter from the convent in Bergamo that hundreds of people were flocking to the shrine. They ripped apart the tree where Mary had been seen, each visitor taking a branch for good luck. The girl in the convent received many articles of clothing and other gifts from people who came to see her. Sr M. Gertrude said proudly that Mary must favor Italy over other countries, since she showed herself there so often. She then listed all the places in Italy where Mary had appeared. I listened carefully and said that I liked to believe in facts.

For the next three weeks, this was the main topic of conversation in the village and especially in our convent. Everybody waited impatiently for the day when Mary would reappear. They even knew when it would happen, down to the hour. Sr Agata gazed at the postcard repeatedly and said that the girl in the picture looked like an angel. I was sure the whole affair was a figment of the girl's imagination. After all, she had reached the age at which she was being prepared to take communion. Stories about saints and miracles, I reasoned, could not but stir the imagination of a youngster who was being taught so many of them, especially in a small village where a child's life is limited to two places, home and church. However, I could not state my opinion openly, even though I knew that some of the nuns were not very enthusiastic about the affair.

The longed-for day arrived. We waited impatiently until 6.00 p.m., the hour when Mary was supposed to appear. When the clock struck six, we gathered in an open field, eyes heavenward, waiting for the miracle to manifest itself. I enjoyed the beautiful sunset. The sky was blue and red. Suddenly, an elderly nun yelled that she saw something in the sky. A second elderly nun near her confirmed it: there was a spot up there. Others strained to look in that direction but saw nothing. One of the young nuns, Sr Pauline, pinched me and whispered in my ear, 'That's funny; these old nuns can hardly see two feet in front of their noses, and now they can see what's in the sky.' I understood her sarcasm and realized that I was the only one to whom she could say this. In general, I knew that the nuns pretended to be more religious and saintly then they really were.

On our way home, one of the day students, Maria, told me that the priest, Don Emanuel, had been standing in the piazza, surrounded by a group of old women and staring at the sky. Suddenly the priest had cried out that he saw Mary. The women genuflected and burst into prayer. Sr M. Gertrude, listening in, was delighted. Not everybody could see Mary, she said, only those who merited it by their deeds. Two days later, we received a letter from the convent in Bergamo: Mary had not appeared that day. The girl was still in the convent. They hoped Mary would tell her when she would reappear. After that, the matter never came up again.

The days passed. The nuns surrounded every visitor to the convent to hear the latest news. Only old Gemma did not care; her whole world was the church and her chickens. As she worked in the chicken coops, she murmured the Ave Maria quietly. Sometimes she stopped me on my way and told me that she had said 20 Ave Marias for me that day. 'Grazie,' I replied. It gave her such pleasure to do something for me.

Gemma was not the only nun who prayed on my behalf. Once, a Sr Carolina told me that she had wished me good luck when she took communion. I thanked her and wondered what she knew about me. Sr Carolina was an art teacher who produced very nice portraits. A reclusive woman who spoke sparingly and quietly, she raised silkworms as a hobby and devoted all her free time to their care and feeding. Only rarely, on summer evenings, would she take us out for a walk in the fields. On those occasions, we talked about various things. Some of the girls spoke of their future and what they expected in life. Sometimes people have the power of prescience, Sr Carolina told us. 'When I was a little girl,' she said, 'I wanted to have a long, wide skirt with big pockets and a bunch of keys to put in them.' She lifted a bunch of keys from her pocket and showed them to us, saying, 'Here they are. Just as I wanted, it came true. It's all from God.' The girls liked to talk with her. She was friendly to them and avoided the rigidity that others displayed. When she was on bedroom duty, the girls maintained strict silence and treated her every word with respect.

Vacation was over. Some of the girls didn't return to the convent because the Allied forces were advancing farther and farther north. They already occupied Rome. The girls' parents kept them at home, not knowing where things might lead. The front was moving in our direction. We often heard the Allies bombing towns and military camps in our vicinity. Whenever we heard the alarm sirens, we ran into the fields and lay in the corn. After someone told us that a low-flying plane had fired its machine gun at cows in the pasture, we stopped going into the fields during air raids. Instead, we hid in the chapel and prayed. The sounds of the aircraft and the exploding bombs terrified us. Sr M. Gertrude was the most frightened of all; her pallor made an especially strong impression. She lifted her eyes to God, praying for our safety. Although I did not doubt the sincerity and strength of her belief in God Almighty and in the eternal life of the soul in Paradise, I could see that she was afraid for her life.

Apart from low-flying craft, we often saw large formations of planes at high altitudes overhead. They were heading to Germany on bombing missions. I stood outside with Anita and counted the planes; they numbered in the hundreds. Sr M. Gertrude, frightened by the very sound of aircraft, ordered us back in. I explained that these planes were only passing by. The sirens hadn't even sounded! She dismissed my explanation; if I was smart enough to understand the danger, she said, I wouldn't stand there watching.

The nuns in Parma decided to pray in their church for three full days, pleading for the war to end on behalf of the suffering people. According to an arrangement they had made, our convent was to pray in the same fashion, also for three days, after the first convent finished its quota. The first two days passed uneventfully, we heard. On the third day, however, a terrible tragedy occurred. The town was bombed and the section of the building that housed the church was struck and totally demolished. Thirteen nuns were killed and many others wounded. It was very hard to remove the casualties from the rubble; meanwhile, those still alive were wailing and moaning.

The news came as a terrible shock to us. The bodies were taken to our convent for burial in a special section of the cemetery for nuns. They were laid on a catafalque, candles were lit, and everybody filed by to pay last respects. The priests and nuns led the funeral procession, followed by the entire population of the village. The people marched in rows, women in one and men in another, reciting the Requiem

Eterna prayer all the way. After the burial, Sr M. Gertrude showed me the graves of all the nuns who were buried there. Back in my room, I lay sprawled on my bed in tears and shock. My memory carried me back to my dear family. They didn't even have gravestones. It was all the result of a war that one madman had brought upon humanity. Innocent adults and children were being killed every day. Hospitals were full of patients who would never be whole again. This war should be remembered. I was sure that all countries that had suffered from it would remember it forever and do everything to prevent another one. For the past five years, so many countries had been waging a terrific struggle to defeat Hitler's barbaric army. When would it end?

Christmas Eve neared. This time, most of the girls stayed in the convent for Christmas vacation. The roads were not safe enough for them to go home. Their parents sent them packages of home-baked sweets and other things. Some even came to visit. None of the girls forgot that I was an orphan alone there. I would open my drawer to find sweets, cakes, or fruit that they had put there for me. Once, to my surprise, I even found some money.

For a long time that winter, I worked with Sr M. Gertrude mending summer dresses that had been washed for use the next summer. We also talked politics. The German forces were retreating on all fronts. I told her that I had not yet made any plans for my postwar life. Don't worry, Sr M. Gertrude said. 'We'll help you with everything. I want to have you near me. I want you to live here in the village, so I can see you often.' She really meant it, I thought. I felt very bad because I could not promise to honor her request, although I would always do my best to see her often, come what may. Sr M. Gertrude was my best friend, the only person who took such care of me. She wanted me to feel like all other girls, without a sense of inferiority or indebtedness. She even gave me a silver necklace that someone had presented to her and told me to give it, as my own, to Maria, the day student. She regularly brought gifts for me to keep, too, and invited me to her house. To round out my wardrobe, she made me a lovely rabbit-fur collar for the coat that I had brought from Poland.

The partisans now often came down from the hills to obtain food from the peasants. Sometimes they went from house to house to collect clothes and blankets. They visited our convent and 'requisitioned' a typewriter, promising to return it after the war. A priest who was in the hills with the partisans visited our convent whenever he was in the area. He was our source of the latest news. We heard that the Italian Fascists were escorting the Germans into the hills to hunt for partisans. They seldom found any. The peasants, eager to help the partisans, advised them of the movements of Germans in the vicinity. They also sheltered anyone who fought against the Germans.

The country was in chaos. There were stories about brothers fighting each other because they were affiliated with different political parties. Shops were empty, food was hard to obtain even for money. People were hungry and angry at the government. The government could do nothing to improve the situation because the Germans had looted the country's reserves and hauled them to Germany for their own people.

Meanwhile, the Allies were advancing on all fronts. In one of his speeches, Hitler tried to rally his people. Victory would be ours, he said; we have a secret weapon that we are about to unleash. Then we'll regain our momentum. Nobody believed him anymore. The Allies' victory was in sight. Whenever I heard about the coming victory, however, I felt a terrible pain in my heart. If only it had happened earlier, my parents might have survived. Now I was alone in the world. The others, all the others, were gone. My only hope was my oldest brother, Imek, who had enlisted with the Russians in 1941, but I had heard nothing from him. The rest of my family had been murdered. I knew the exact dates of their transports.

After Christmas, three nuns from another convent were transferred to our institution. One of them, Sr Camilla, was about 30 years of age. The others were much older. I noticed that Sr Camilla spent much of her time alone, either praying in the church or walking in the field in her free time. A few days after her arrival, we got to know each other well. From our conversations, I understood that she was very unhappy. She had less to say than the other nuns about eternal life and saints. Then I saw her walking by herself on the interior road. When I approached her, she dried her face and eyes, as if she had been crying. She had taken off her thick glasses; now, as I came up beside her, she put them back on. She asked me if I would do her a great favor and tell no one about it. She knew I would be going to Parma the next day to make some arrangements for the convent. Would I deliver a letter to her sister? I agreed to do it. She handed me the sealed envelope. I returned to my room and placed it in my drawer.

Before I left for Parma, Sr M. Gertrude helped me work out final details and pack. Under the circumstances, I couldn't take the letter out of my drawer without arousing suspicion. I told her that I had to go back to the dining room and pack some food. I ran through the dining room, went to my bedroom, took the letter from my drawer, returned to the dining room, and hid the letter between two slices of bread. Then I ran straight to the bus station, where the bus to Parma was about to leave. Hurriedly I bade goodbye to Sr M. Gertrude and boarded the bus. I was relieved when the bus pulled away.

I thought of Sr Camilla all the way to Parma. Why was she so unhappy? My first stop after getting off in Parma was Sr Camilla's sister. She lived far from the bus terminal; I had to take a streetcar and then walk for several blocks along narrow streets until I came to a stone house that bore the right number. I knocked on the door. A young woman opened the door for me and asked me to step in. I introduced myself and told her that I had a letter from her sister.

'Another letter?' she said. Apparently this letter was not the first of its kind. 'My sister doesn't take into account that she's not so young and pretty anymore. She's had eye trouble. After being in a convent for 15 years, she doesn't have friends here anymore. What does she think she would do here, especially in wartime? I myself have a husband and two children here. My husband doesn't earn enough for me to support her. She ought to realize this herself. If she leaves the convent, she won't find the world that she imagines. I'm sure she won't find her happiness here, either.'

I listened carefully. When she finished, I told her that she must help her sister somehow. Maybe she could convince her to change her mind. The woman responded with an angry silence. I walked away, felling sorry for Sr Camilla. I was becoming more and more aware that convent life had problems of its own that outsiders could not appreciate. As an insider, I had been able to study quite a few nuns. Each, I saw, had personal problems. Very few were truly content with their lives.

Then I remembered something. An older man from the village near my convent used to come by to fix the plumbing in the kitchen. One day, the Mother Superior approached him as he worked and told him that it was not too late to change his attitude toward God. Confess all your sins, she urged, and God will forgive you. You must believe in God and save your soul. The man laughed at her, saying that he believed neither in God nor in the eternity of the soul. An older nun standing near them burst into tears. 'How dare you say a thing like that?' she said. 'I've offered my whole life to God and here you say that God doesn't exist!' I tried to console the weeping nun by telling her that the man hadn't really meant it. I felt so sorry for her. That man had nearly ruined her whole world with his words.

Back in the convent, I found Sr Camilla waiting to know whether I had delivered her letter. I said nothing about my conversation with her sister. The next day I went back to work with Sr M. Gertrude, still thinking about my talk with Sr Camilla's sister. I asked Sr M. Gertrude if there was really no way to help a nun who had spent 15 years of her life in the convent but no longer felt at home there. Such a woman found everything in the convent burdensome and could no longer endure that life, I added. In response, Sr M. Gertrude explained that there was a special period in every nun's life that she had to overcome. The Devil worked his way under her skin and poisoned her with doubt. She had to apply strong willpower to exorcise him. The priest could help her to do it, but only if she confessed to him.

I understood that this conversation would not get me very far. How fortunate believers were, I thought. How helpful their faith was in their lives. Sr M. Gertrude continued to tell me about eternal life in the afterworld, the commandments, and how Christ and the saints had suffered. None of it convinced me that Sr Camilla should continue to endure convent life against the dictates of her feelings. Then I told Sr M. Gertrude whom I was talking about. What, for instance, I asked, would become of Sr Camilla? When the war ended, Sr M. Gertrude replied, she might be sent to a convent in Switzerland, far away from her sister. Perhaps then she would feel better and change her mind.

With no newspapers at hand, I had almost no way of knowing what was going on in the world. My only regular outside contacts were villagers who visited the convent. They knew and cared little about events outside their village. By this time, we wanted to hear every day where the Allied forces were. We asked everyone who came in from the village for the latest news. All we received were word of mouth rumors and miscellaneous stories. We did learn, however, that the partisans were in contact with the Allies and received supplies from them by air. Many of the partisan forces were fighting together with the Allies against their common enemy. The beginning of May was the most exciting time for us. Now we knew for sure that the war would end within days, if not hours. One morning, the bells at the gate rang loudly and uninterruptedly. I ran out of the kitchen to find out what it meant. Maria stood in the yard, surrounded by nuns, all talking loudly and happily. 'The war is over!' Maria announced. '*Pace, pace!*' She grabbed my arm and pulled me into the street. Partisans had come in from the hills and gathered on the piazza. People mobbed and kissed them.

At that moment, Maria spotted her brother among the

partisans. She ran to greet him. Friends of theirs surrounded them. I stood alone. Nobody paid any attention to me. I stared at all the people. They were happy now. This was the moment they had been waiting for. I had also been waiting for it for so long, but now that it had arrived, I realized how alone I was in the world.

Instead of waiting for Maria to come back, I ran to the convent and lay down on my bed. I was not so thrilled with the peace. I felt an inner emptiness. I had nobody to embrace and kiss, nobody whose homecoming I could look forward to. I came to the conclusion that in addition to the millions whom Hitler and his barbaric murderers had killed, the survivors, like myself, were so deeply hurt that our wounds would never heal.

NOTES

1. After Poland was occupied in September 1939, young Jews fled toward the Soviet border and crossed into Soviet territory.
2. A Polish town in the Soviet occupation zone that had a Jewish population of more than 17,000. The Germans occupied it in June 1941 and established a ghetto there. In July 1942, the Jewish population was deported to the Belzec extermination camp.
3. The Soviet secret police.
4. The Ukrainian Nationalist Organization (Orhanizatsya Ukrainskikh Nationalistiv, OUN), which aspired to political independence. It did the Germans' bidding in the hope that the Germans would award the Ukrainians a state of their own. In 1940, the organization splintered and an extreme faction was established under the leadership of Stefan Bandera.
5. The secret police in Nazi Germany.
6. Rabbi Ezekiel Levin was the spiritual leader of the Progressive Jewish congregation in Lwów. He turned down an offer to hide in a convent and was arrested and murdered while returning to his congregation.
7. 'Jew,' 'swine.'
8. One of the decrees against the Jews was the wearing of a badge of shame on their clothing or on their arms. The device chosen in Lwów was a white armband imprinted with a blue Star of David.
9. The Nazis decreed the establishment of Judenräte in towns that had sizable Jewish populations as part of their web of concealment and deception.
10. A town in eastern Poland with a Jewish population of 15,000. It was captured by the Soviets at the beginning of the war but the Soviet army retreated on 9 October 1939, and several hundred Jews fled with it.
11. Yom Kippur is the holiest day on the Jewish calendar – a day of forgiveness and absolution among individuals and between individuals and their God.
12. The Jews were driven out of their homes in Lwów and concentrated in a special

neighborhood at the edge of town – a rundown, wretched slum quarter.

13. In regard to the Janowska camp, see the Introduction.
14. There were several workshops and a milling machinery factory on Janowska Street. The Germans used the location as a central place for building materials and established new waste recycling workshops, carpentry shops, and other enterprises there.
15. Several Italian units reached Lwów together with the Germans as part of Italy's participation in the war at Germany's side. In the main, they performed service and maintenance duties. Many soldiers in these units wrote home and expressed their horror over the persecution of the Jews.
16. The 'Aryan' area – the part of town where Poles and Ukrainians lived.
17. Jews employed in enterprises that manufactured for German industry were issued with special labor permits that often saved their lives when abductions and Aktionen took place.
18. On 21 August 1942, an order was issued for the establishment of a ghetto in the cramped area of the Jewish quarter. The ghetto was surrounded with a wooden fence and only one gate, guarded by Ukrainian sentries, served as a crossing.
19. A town in eastern Poland with a Jewish population of 17,000. It was occupied on 2 July 1941, and a ghetto was established there. Shortly afterwards, most of the Jews were transported to the Belzec camp for extermination.
20. A regulation that the Germans promulgated, according to which Jewish workers were sorted by two criteria: R – Rustung Industrie, workers in industrial plants, and W, those who worked for the Wehrmacht.
21. The German army.
22. A prayer recited by the bereaved for deceased relatives.
23. An ethnic minority of German origin that lived in Poland.
24. In the Warsaw ghetto uprising, which broke out in April 1943, a small group of young Jews, equipped with firebombs and a few rifles, managed to inflict losses on the Germans, cause them embarrassment, and make them afraid of its effect on Jews in other ghettos. Jews in Lwów, too, attempted to launch an uprising before the ghetto was liquidated.
25. Rawa Ruska, a labor camp established in December 1942. Conditions there were relatively mild because the Germans used the camp for propaganda and deception purposes. Liquidated in June 1942.
26. A *Kenkarte,* a certificate issued to the Jews in the ghetto.
27. An airfield where Jews had worked was discovered in Sknilów, near Lwów.
28. In Italian: Jew.
29. Vienna Station.